I SURRENDER
ALL

Other Books by Priscilla Shirer

One in a Million: Journey to Your Promised Land

Life Interrupted: Navigating the Unexpected

The Resolution for Women

God Is Able

*Fervent: A Woman's Battle Plan for Serious,
Specific, and Strategic Prayer*

Awaken: 90 Days with the God Who Speaks

Discerning the Voice of God

He Speaks to Me

A Jewel in His Crown

For Younger Readers

The Prince Warriors (book 1 in The Prince Warriors series)

The Prince Warriors and the Unseen Invasion (book 2)

The Prince Warriors and the Swords of Rhema (book 3)

The Winter War (book 4)

Unseen: The Prince Warriors 365 Devotional

Radiant: His Light, Your Life

Inspired by the themes of the feature film THE FORGE

I SURRENDER ALL

PRISCILLA SHIRER

B&H
PUBLISHING®
BRENTWOOD, TENNESSEE

979-8-3845-0526-6

Published by B&H Publishing Group
Brentwood, Tennessee

Dewey Decimal Classification: 248.84
Subject Heading: CHRISTIAN LIFE /
EVANGELISTIC WORK / CONVERT

Cover design and illustration by Rafael Nobre, Good
Illustration LTD. Author photo by Kariss Farris.

1 2 3 4 5 6 7 • 28 27 26 25 24

To John and Trina Jenkins

Thank you for being His disciples.
And for discipling us.
We are forever grateful.

Contents

All or Nothing

Many years ago, I traveled from my home in central Texas to upstate Connecticut to speak at a conference. I honestly don't remember much about the event itself. It's been more than twenty years. But my memory about the place where I stayed for those three days remains crystal clear.

You'll see why.

There were four of us altogether, all the speakers for the weekend, waiting at the airport baggage claim area when a van arrived to pick us up and take us to our accommodations. Light snow was falling as a member of the conference committee hopped out to greet us and welcome us to town. After we put our bags inside and each of us had taken our seats, she turned to us and told us where we were headed.

She excitedly said that in lieu of a hotel, a local resident who was on the board of the organization had generously agreed to welcome us into her home.

Hmm. This was different. But okay. We all chatted cheerily with one another during the twenty-minute drive from the airport while our host regaled us with descriptions of what this incredible house was like. Still, when we rounded the final bend and saw it for ourselves, we gasped audibly. Blank stares passed between us for a moment, as if perhaps at this last turn in the road, we'd left the real world behind and been escorted into a fairy tale.

Sprawling out before us was a vast estate surrounded by towering trees with meticulously manicured shrubbery lining the entrance, dusted in snow. The house itself was—well, they said we wouldn't be staying at a hotel, but this three-story mansion looked as big and luxurious as any five-star property I'd ever seen.

We were still trying to absorb the spectacle of it all when our van curved to a stop along the circular driveway, underneath a porte cochere supported by large marble pillars, where the lady of the house stood in the doorway waiting to welcome us. The four of us exchanged glances and sideways smiles inside the van before exiting, in disbelief that we'd be staying here, in this gorgeous home that was truly beyond our expectation.

The woman waiting for us could not have been more gracious and inviting. She was as warm, humble, and endearing as her surroundings were grand. She hugged us sincerely one by one as we stepped down out of the van, and then she helped us carry our things inside. *Inside.*

Twenty-thousand square feet opened up before us like the breaking of the sun over the horizon on a crisp summer day. The "Hallelujah Chorus" sung by a host of angels echoed around us. (Or was that just in my head?) Pristine. Polished. Palatial. Perfect. We weren't sure exactly what to do next, but as we stood together gawking inside the front door, our host gave us our first instructions. She asked if we'd be willing, before walking any further into the house, to kindly remove our shoes.

Sure, of course. I mean, if I lived in a place as impeccable and immaculate as this, I'd probably ask people not to clomp around in their dirty shoes through my house either. But no sooner had she led us a few steps forward than she asked if we'd mind also not walking on the massive, handwoven European rug that lay across the floor of the entryway. She explained to us that this tapestry, a one-of-its-kind design, had been imported from a remote province and that she didn't allow either her family or her guests to walk on it, ever.

A rug. In the middle of the floor. That no one walked on.

So we compliantly shuffled around the edges, being careful to restrict our movements to the hardwood floor that created a narrow walking margin. Soon we arrived inside another room, the living room, equally expansive, featuring floor-to-ceiling windows that provided a majestic view of the back acreage. Just beyond was a connected

hallway that contained its own elevator for conveying
people up and down the three levels of the house.

With the click of a button, the doors slid open, and
the woman motioned us to step inside. But carefully,
please. As we entered with our bags in tow, she called
our attention to the burnished slats of wood, elaborately
carved, that ringed the interior of the elevator car. This
wood, not unlike the rug, had been shipped from India
while the home was being built, and she was glad to say
she'd succeeded so far in keeping it from being chipped or
damaged. She asked us to be mindful of our baggage so it
wouldn't scrape the walls.

Imagine how tightly we then gripped our purses and
carry-ons, tucking our belongings underneath our arms
as the door opened on the third level. We gingerly exited
in a neat single file.

Here is where we would be staying and sleeping for
the weekend, each of us in our own separate master
bedroom containing a king-size bed, sitting area, and
private bath. I gently set my suitcase on the floor as our
host was showing the others to their living quarters and
was just about to sit down on the bed when she appeared
again and said, "Oh, excuse me, before you sit, would you
mind allowing me to fold up the comforter that's on the
bed? We don't actually sleep with those. They're only for
decoration." Even as she spoke the words, she was already
gathering up the bedspread, which she then precisely

folded and tucked away neatly inside the closet, repeating the process for all of us.

Whew! We'd made it. From the front door all the way up here to these spacious bedroom suites, without touching anything or upsetting anything, in our sock-clad feet. Relieved by this, I think, our genial hostess turned elegantly to face us, thanked us again so much for coming, and said,

"Make yourself at home!"

What irony! Make ourselves at home? Here? Really? When shoes can't be worn? Rugs can't be walked on? Knickknacks can't be touched? Certain rooms can't be entered? Walls can't be leaned against? And comforters can't be comforting?

She'd been so kind to let us stay here, and all of us were so thankful for her genuine hospitality. More than that, the warmth I'd seen in her eyes and heart made me feel an instant affection for her. We all felt the same way. But her invitation for us to "make ourselves at home," wasn't an offer we could truly relax into. Because, let's be honest, she clearly didn't mean for us to feel *too much* at home. There were clear boundaries and limitations, certain areas and certain treasures we knew we couldn't touch.

Invite us in? Yes.

Give us unhindered access to everything? Absolutely not.

Many of us as believers in Christ have been known to treat our Savior this same way. We've invited Him in. We're glad He's here. We like having Him close, and we like considering Him a friend. We enjoy His company, even going so far as to give Him a choice room in our heart where He can stay. We've said, in essence, "Savior, make Yourself at home in me," but what we really mean is, "Savior, you are welcome in *some* places." We'll let Him be here within limits and give Him entrée to certain general areas. But there are other spaces of our lives to which we have no intention of giving Him unfettered access, and there are treasures inside we don't really want Him to disturb.

- Ambitions He's not allowed to touch
- Entertainment choices He's not allowed to overrule
- Comforts we hold dear that He's not allowed to influence
- Opinions and perspectives He's not allowed to sway
- Family traditions He's not allowed to upend
- Relationships He's not allowed to undo
- Attitudes He's not allowed to shift
- Subjects He's not allowed to address
- Dreams He's not allowed to challenge

- Expectations He's not allowed to adjust
- Financial priorities He's not allowed to guide
- Career goals He's not allowed to alter

We're afraid that surrendering the whole of ourselves to Him, giving Him full access to our entire lives, will cause disruptions to our preferred way of living our lives. We fear His intrusive touch might disorder the life we've built or are trying to build. We're uncomfortable thinking He might go around looking into places we've intentionally hidden from view. We're avoidant of the work He might require of us if He finds something that needs adjustment or renovation, perhaps even a complete overhaul. We do not want His purifying gaze of conviction roaming freely throughout the home of our hearts, our minds, our emotions, and our actions. So we say to Him, in essence . . .

Come in as *Savior*.

But not as *Lord*.

Here lies the thin line of demarcation that separates the *believer* from the *disciple*. The *saved* life from the *surrendered* life. Believing is where we begin: repenting of our sins, receiving His forgiveness. Welcoming Him in. Salvation happens in that moment. But being His disciple is the road we then start traveling. Every day. For the rest of our lives. And it's the only road—the narrow road—that leads us where we really want to go.

The disciple has chosen to surrender her all. To release control. To give unhindered access to every part of her life—all of it—to the One who paid the exorbitant price to redeem her life in the first place. To the disciple, Christ is not a visitor held at a cautious arm's length who enters on a restricted basis, answerable to her demands. He is instead a Ruler who possesses full authority to reorient the disciple's life so that it aligns with His purposes, both for her and for His glory.

He is the builder of this house and its chief Cornerstone. The disciple recognizes He is the actual Owner, and she is the steward. He is the Maker of this relationship. And He is the Lover of her soul, whose desire it is to turn this life she lives into something He can work through and use to make a deep, transformative impact on her world for His kingdom. At times, she's worried about the high cost of a life like this. In different seasons, she felt like running from it, fighting hard against it. But she's discovered, to her joy, she never wants to go back. Because no other life can match the disciple's life.

The surrendered life.

So she keeps surrendering all. Even the parts she treasures most. She brings her whole self to Him each morning, every area, every element of what the Bible calls her "everyday, ordinary life—your sleeping, eating, going-to-work, and walking-around life." She places it before God "as an offering." She's learned, as so many others have, not to "become so well-adjusted to your culture that you fit into it without even thinking. Instead, fix your attention on God. You'll be changed from the inside out. Readily recognize what he wants from you, and quickly respond to it. Unlike the culture around you, always dragging you down to its level of immaturity, God brings the best out of you, develops well-formed maturity in you" (Rom. 12:1–2 MSG).

Her eyes are fixed on Jesus. The culture is not her authority. *He* is.

Because she is His disciple.

꿍

The idea of being a disciple was already in existence in the ancient world before Jesus came. All throughout the Old Testament, in ancient Jewish society, the importance and implications of discipleship were conveyed to God's people, even though the word itself wasn't used. They were commanded to "walk in his ways" (Deut. 30:16), to "be holy because I am holy" (Lev. 11:44), and were frequently warned against patterning their lives after pagan deities and committing their allegiance to them. The actual term *disciple* was first used to describe students of Greek philosophers like Aristotle and Plato, who sought to revolutionize the culture around them, including Jewish culture, with Greek thought and influence.

These philosophers knew their pupils could never glean the depth of insight required to shift an entire civilization merely by intellectual training. Cultivating *knowledgeable* students was not their ultimate aim. They wanted much more than mental enlightenment. They wanted their learners to absorb this new way of life so deeply into their being that it transformed the way they thought about and lived their whole lives.

- The way they worked.
- The political perspectives they held.
- The financial shrewdness they employed.
- The family structure they built.
- The entertainment choices they enjoyed.
- The words they exchanged.
- The priorities they pursued.
- The education they valued.
- The disciplines they practiced.

So students of Greek philosophy became "disciples"— apprentices who immersed their whole selves not only into listening to what they were being taught but also by observing the one who taught them. So they tethered their lives to their teacher and they left everything to follow him. They followed him into his home. They watched how he interacted with others and how he governed his behavior in public and private spheres. They observed and absorbed his habits and disciplines, with the sole purpose of replicating the life of their mentor and making the character and cadence of his life their own. Their goal was not merely to learn things, to build up a knowledge base, but to become a fully formed copy of their teacher not just by embracing his ideas but by identifying with him and imitating him in every way, in every aspect of their lives.

This book you're reading is a call—an invitation—to that kind of radical relationship with Jesus. To be His disciple. To be a true follower. To become a fully formed copy of the Teacher.

This pursuit *includes* being a student, of course, learning about Him through His Word so that our minds are renewed and shaped by truth. But it's far more involved than that—more intimate, more all-inclusive, more of an investment, truly a full integration of ourselves with Him. Just as the ancient Greeks understood, this kind of relationship cannot develop in a two-hour meeting, once a week. It can't just be a Sunday morning thing. It's a whole-life, Sunday-to-Saturday, daily surrendering and aligning of all we are to all He is, until we start to look exactly like our Teacher.

- In how we speak
- In how we behave
- In the restraint we exhibit
- In the humility we exude
- In the kindness we share

- In the perspectives we have
- In the choices we make
- In the priorities we maintain

Please know, if you feel a sense of resistance or hesitation to this kind of all-in surrender, to authentic discipleship—feeling it's too hard, too complicated, too intrusive, or will leave you too out of control of your own life—you are not alone. The whole rhythm and pattern of this world, not to mention the nature of our flesh, resists the submission that a wholehearted following of Jesus requires. But at its essence, this lifestyle is not a more complicated life. It's an invitation to receive a gift of simplicity and freedom.

No, it isn't easy. It is indeed costly. But somehow the grace and goodness of God have made this experience of discipleship freeing and simplifying, getting all the parts of our lives headed in one direction. In His direction. Hear Him whisper to your hesitancy, "Come to Me, all who are weary and burdened, and I will give you rest. Take My yoke upon you and learn from Me, for I am gentle and humble in heart, and you will find rest for your souls" (Matt. 11:28–29 NASB).

Rest. For your soul.

Surrender is how you finally find it.

I believe you probably picked up this book because, like me, you want to experience the fullness and abundance our faith is designed to offer. You want more. More peace, more balance. More power, more momentum. More of an impact on people around you. More satisfaction, more contentment. More hope, more joy. More love coming out of you, more love coming in to carry you. More courage to keep going.

The surrounding culture will try to convince you that the only way to find these things is by pursuing each one of them outright. But Jesus tells you that "all these things will be added to you" when you do one surrendered thing—"seek first the kingdom of God and his righteousness" (Matt. 6:33 ESV). As a disciple.

Jesus has it all.

And He has it all to give.

But first, He must have all of you.

If there's a single idea that I hope becomes hardwired into our heads as we journey along together, it's "all," it's "everything." *I Surrender All.* The whole house and everything in it. Because *all* is where the life is. *All* is where the meaning is. *All* is what He requires, and *all* is what He deserves.

All the things.

Everything.

༄

This book has eight chapters, and I've intentionally titled each of them around the word "Everything." I've repeated it and echoed it because *everything*, indeed, is the crux of what the invitation to discipleship demands. Expect it to be challenging because Jesus Himself said it would be.

> "If anyone wants to follow after me, let him deny himself, take up his cross, and follow me." (Matt. 16:24)

There's an "all" and an "everything" to what He's saying.

> "For whoever wants to save his life will lose it; but whoever loses his life for My sake will find it. For what good will it do a person if he gains the whole world, but forfeits his soul?" (Matt. 16:25–26 NASB)

So this is serious. To "lose" your life, to "surrender" your life, all of it, is an enormous ask. But not if it's the only way to "find" your life—fulfillment, contentment, and purpose.

In order to help you digest and internalize what you're reading and then be able to recall what the Holy Spirit is teaching you, I've included a section at the end of each chapter for you and your Savior to talk with each other and savor the new depths of your relationship. It's designed to help you actively process what surrendering to the Lord means. Because if this experience we're embarking on is going to be complete, we can't just read about it. We need to *do something* about it. More accurately, we need to let Him do something in us. We must kneel before Him, surrendering to Him.

And when we reach the end of the book, I'm going to ask the Lord to align your life with someone else—a spiritually mature, Spirit-filled, wise, and compassionate follower of Jesus—who can continue to walk with you, encourage you, correct you, challenge you. *Disciple you.* In fact, I wonder if you looked carefully you might discover there's already someone in your sphere of influence right now who has taken seriously His command to "go, therefore, and make disciples" (Matt. 28:19). We all need people like this in our life, in a personal and intimate way—someone who will take our hand, walk with us in grace, encourage us toward deeper spiritual maturity in the practical areas of living, and then show us how we can become a disciple maker as well.

This is how change and transformation begin to happen, when we walk with others and when they walk with us. All of us, bringing all of ourselves, into all the things He wants to do through us.

So here we go. I could not be more delighted you're here. Take His hand with me—chapter by chapter, page by page, moment by special moment—and let's follow Him together.

All the way.

All-in.
Always.
With everything.
I Surrender All.

CHAPTER 1

Everything You Have

They brought the boats to land,
left everything, and followed him.

Luke 5:11

Mrs. Wright was my second-grade teacher, and every day she wore the same thing: an ankle-length hoop skirt, cinched at the waist, gathered into folds at the bottom. I can still hear the *swish* of that fabric when she'd brush past our desks handing out papers.

She apparently only owned three of those skirts in all because the rotation was as clockwork as her weekly math quizzes. She had a solid cream one, a navy blue one, and a black one, always paired with coordinating blouses. Nicely patterned. Button-down.

As for the rest of her appearance, she wore her dark black hair tightly curled by roller set. It no doubt required a full hour or more under a steamy hair dryer. She then cemented this conservative style into place with a healthy dose of hair spray that covered every strand in a shiny film.

Her makeup was smooth, clean, impeccable—just enough, not too much. The only bit of daring was how she curled up her eyeliner at the ends, creating that enchanted cat-eyed look.

That was Mrs. Wright of the second grade. And I couldn't imagine her looking any other way because it's the only way I'd ever seen her. My seven-year-old mind just never contemplated this woman doing anything else but teaching school or existing anywhere other than our classroom. This was the totality of her—this place, this look. One-dimensional. My friends and I, on the other hand, had full lives like regular people. We went home and did other things, in other clothes, around other people. But not Mrs. Wright. Not the long, homely hoop skirt. To us, her teacher life was the only dimension she occupied.

Which is why my world was rocked, one hot Texas Saturday afternoon, tagging along with my mom on a grocery store run. We were queuing up in the checkout line. I was scanning the forbidden enticements of the candy rack when, with one casual turn, I instantly felt my body freeze into a statue position. Wide eyes. Open mouth.

Mrs. Wright was there. At the grocery store. On a weekend. And her hair wasn't coiffed up rigidly on her head but was loose and free, falling romantically around her shoulders. Her face was rosy, natural, except for a hint of lip gloss, maybe the faintest trace of blush. And . . .

Wait. What was this? *Shorts? Legs?*

Where did these legs come from?

I was baffled. Mrs. Wright owned shorts? And knees?

And apparently a family. She and her bare legs were just standing there at the cash register, completely out of context—completely out of her skirts—next to a man I assumed to be her husband, along with a young boy I assumed to be her son.

Mrs. Wright had a . . . life?

Thinking back on this incident forty years later, I can't remember if I even spoke to her or not. I was too dumbfounded to utter a human word (which for me, even then, was saying something). This was the day—*the very first day*—that I realized Mrs. Wright was more than just a teacher. She was a whole woman. She had a multidimensional life. She was a wife and mother who bought groceries on Saturday, probably went to church on Sunday, took walks around her neighborhood, and went out for brunch with her friends, in addition to teaching us silly second-graders on the weekdays. I could not have been more shocked.

Did I mention she had knees?

Up to that point, if you had asked me, "Who do you say Mrs. Wright is?," my answer would've been narrow, simplistic, and one-dimensional. A teacher. That's it. My summary of her identity would've valued her as much less than the whole person I now could see and understand her to be. But if I had known her better, if I'd ever seen her as more than what the other kids and I just assumed her to be by elementary observation, it would've changed some things. Limiting her to my narrow perspective—as just a nice, good teacher—didn't limit her; it just limited my relationship with her, how I responded to her and interacted with her.

⌒

In Luke 9:20, Jesus asked His disciples, "Who do you say that I am?" He was alone with them, praying with them (perhaps praying *for* them), when he turned to present the question and receive their reply.

Let me set the context. By this time in their journey with Him, He'd already revealed a lot about who He was. The first eight chapters of Luke's Gospel leading up to this moment provide so many explanations and implications about the full identity of Jesus:

- The stunning announcement of His coming (chapter 1)
- The supernatural nature of His birth (chapter 2)
- The confirmation of His deity, the Son of God (chapter 3)
- The way He thwarted the enemy's attempt at derailing His mission (chapter 4)

- The miracles that authenticated His messiahship (chapter 5)
- The noticeable depth and difference of His teaching (chapter 6)
- The startling display of His compassion for sinners (chapter 7)
- The power of His command over creation and over evil (chapter 8)

And these are just the high points. This whole section of Scripture cements the identity of Jesus, replete with convincing and comprehensive evidence declaring Him to be exactly who He claimed to be.

He was not just a newborn baby. He existed before time began, the Creator of His own mother.

He was not just an average kid wandering around the temple. He was at home in His Father's house, tending to "My Father's business" (Luke 2:49 NKJV).

He was not just a man being baptized in the Jordan. He was the one upon whom "the Holy Spirit descended," whose Father called out to Him from heaven, "You are my beloved Son; with you I am well-pleased" (Luke 3:22).

He was not just someone whose perfect character drew Satan's eye, to be seduced into abandoning His ministerial assignment. He was the one upon whom the redemption of humanity rested, the one of whom the prophets testified, the one anointed to "preach good news to the poor" and to "proclaim release to the captives" (Luke 4:18).

He was not just a helpless bystander hearing about and becoming overwhelmed by people's sickness and lack. He was the architect of the universe, able to heal and restore, to banish demons back to hell, to cause "the winds and the waves" to obey His spoken command (Luke 8:25).

He was not just another religious leader—a mere teacher—seeking to explain the law, and He was certainly not there to use His knowledge of the sacred for self-righteous ends, as so many did. No, He was the "Lord of the Sabbath" (Luke 6:5), the fulfillment of the law Himself, declaring to everyone who would listen that the kingdom of God could be theirs.

So when He asked His disciples, "Who do you say that I am?" in Luke 9, they had already witnessed many startling proofs of His identity in chapters 1–8. *Then* Jesus asked. And their response formed the bedrock upon which the whole issue of their discipleship rested.

Who *is* Jesus?

Only when we have a comprehensive and accurate view of His identity—His deity, His holiness, His authority, His distinctiveness—only then are we willing, even eager, to fully surrender to Him. If our view of Him is distorted or diminished, if it's impotent or anemic—if we think less of Him than He truly is—we will withhold from Him the devotion that rightfully belongs to Him. We will seek a better alternative when we've been hurt by the church, or disappointed by one of its leaders, or when we're grappling with issues of faith amid life's difficult moments. We'll think *we* are our best alternative, that only *we* can be trusted to look out for our own well-being.

If, to us, Jesus is a narrow, one-dimensional religious caricature that we've relegated to the "Sunday school" part of our lives, it makes sense that we'd hold ourselves back from Him. Why would anyone choose to tether their lives to someone they don't fully trust? Why would anyone surrender their future to someone they don't have confidence in? Why would anyone relinquish the reins of control to a God they don't truly believe to be sovereign, omniscient, all-powerful, and all-good? If in our opinion He is less than what we need our Lord to be, then He doesn't have the credibility to command our full attention, to be worth risking our lives on.

What I'm saying is this: if you and I are struggling to surrender our all to Jesus, it most likely has something to do with our estimation of His identity. We're not seeing Him as He truly is. We're confining Him to church or to Christmas or to spiritual words we're supposed to say.

If we're only giving Him the parts we think we can spare, it's because we've relegated Him to a one-dimensional existence, like Mrs. Wright in the classroom.

We've limited Him to the few places where we think He belongs.

We've made Him too small for us to follow, too small for our complete surrender.

Because who would turn their lives over to someone who is just "a good teacher"?

During Jesus's earthly ministry, most people never thought of following Him the way the twelve disciples did. That's because most people, for the most part, could never get past thinking of Him mainly as a teacher, an elevated version of "John the Baptist" or "Elijah" or "one of the ancient prophets" come to life (Luke 9:19).

If Jesus had been only that—merely a good teacher—being mentioned alongside these greats could've been viewed as a high-end accolade. But the comparison of Jesus to even these illustrious men of the cloth was nothing short of an insult. He was not a man on par with the esteemed prophets of the past. He hadn't come just to teach about the kingdom of heaven but to inaugurate it, to fulfill it, to be our sovereign Redeemer, the living and dying Son of God. The multitudes may have respected Him. They may have been fascinated by Him. But their watered-down view of His identity would always keep them from walking in close fellowship and proximity with Jesus. In contrast, Peter and the other disciples knew Him to be who He truly said He was—the fully divine, holy Deity, unable to be compared and without counterpart.

The result? They followed Him.

Even as I write this, the piercing yet gentle conviction of the Holy Spirit falls fresh on me. I've been through many seasons of life where, looking back on them now, I can see I viewed the Lord wrongly. I saw Him as small, fragile, distant, and limited. I'd never have admitted it, largely because I didn't realize it. But the hesitancy with which I trusted Him revealed this truth. Whenever I was slow in laying something down—a pleasure I wanted, a position I insisted on holding—whenever I resisted going a certain way or shifting my attitude or perspective as His Word and Spirit directed me, my reluctance to obey Him, to surrender my all to Him, shined a spotlight on something else. Something more. I didn't think He was sovereign enough to trust with the outcome of my future fulfillment.

Can you relate? Every dogged commitment we make to our own paths and ambitions, to our own choices, to our own deeply held desires for personal autonomy and independence, says we think more highly of ourselves than we do of Him. We trust ourselves more. We trust our ideas more. We trust in our efforts and achievements more. Perhaps we trust another person more. But Jesus? Can we trust Him? He may be a lot, but He's not quite enough, not if we've watered Him down to a Teacher we listen to but not a Master we fully submit to.

౨౨

None of us comes naturally to this comprehensive, all-inclusive belief about who Jesus is and to the full surrender that discipleship requires.

Neither did Simon Peter.

The only thing we know about Peter, the first time we meet him in Scripture (when he went only by the name of Simon), was that he was an experienced fisherman. But even people with a great deal of experience at doing something can come up against situations they're not expecting.

In Luke 5 (well before Jesus asked the disciples about their view of His identity), Peter and his crew had been out all night in the Sea of Galilee, confident in their nautical abilities and their knowledge about the best conditions for hauling in a decent catch. Again and again, they had cast their cumbersome net over the side of the boat, expecting it to return to them filled to the brim with fish, like it always did. But to their surprise, every attempt came up empty. Every swing was a miss. The waters appeared to be unoccupied tonight. None of the fishermen's keen insights was paying off.

Picture the difficulty and discouragement they must have felt as each dark hour dovetailed into the next. Imagine their bewilderment at not being able to do a job they'd successfully performed hundreds of times before.

Fishing wasn't just their weekend hobby. Fishing was their career—the industry and craft to which they had dedicated their lives. Failing to catch a single fish on an all-night endeavor would've meant more than a disappointment. It was an affront to their skill and expertise, to their esteem as professionals, not to mention a hindrance to their economic bottom line. Their families and communities were counting on these men to bring home the next day's meal. Their overnight failure would not go undetected.

The next morning, the crowds were already out in force, listening to Jesus teach "God's word" (Luke 5:1)—a biblical phrase that, whenever it appears in the Gospels, refers to His teaching about Himself as the Messiah, the bringer of good news. In other words, He was teaching about His identity. And the people were pressing in so tightly to listen that He needed a better platform if He was going to be able to talk where everyone could hear Him.

Eyeing Simon's boat sitting empty on the beach—not a coincidence—He called out to him while the men was washing their empty nets. Again, not a coincidence, because Simon's emptiness was about to be filled by Christ's presence and power. Jesus stepped onto the empty platform of that boat and asked the fishermen to push out a little way from the shore so He could teach the crowds gathered around the water's edge more effectively. From there, Simon would've had the closest seat in the house. He was front and center, next to Jesus, to hear with startling clarity what Jesus continued to say about who He was and about His messianic identity.

Then he heard something else. Something more. Something personal. He heard his name.

Simon?

> "Put out into deep water and let down your
> nets for a catch." (v. 4)

This sentiment went against everything an experienced fisherman knew about working in this area. To effectively fish the Sea of Galilee, traditionally you stayed in the shallow water, fishing at night, not in the deep part in bright daylight. Peter initially tried to reason with Jesus, presenting his bona fides as a man who knew the fishing business better than some Teacher did. They'd worked all night and caught nothing, he said. Jesus didn't answer. Jesus waited.

Okay then, "If you say so, I'll let down the nets," (v. 5). *But I'm telling you, it won't do any good.*

> When they did this, they caught a great
> number of fish, and their nets began to
> tear. So they signaled to their partners in
> the other boat to come and help them; they

came and filled both boats so full that they
began to sink. (vv. 6–7)

Now we come to the best part.

When Simon Peter saw this, he fell at Jesus's
knees and said, "Go away from me, because
I am a sinful man, Lord!" (v. 8)

Not just Teacher. "Lord."

For he and all those with him were amazed
at the catch of fish they had taken, and so
were James and John, Zebedee's sons, who
were Simon's partners. (vv. 9–10)

As recently as the morning's sunrise, Jesus had seemed
to them no more than a local teacher, a religious man who
taught by the seashore. But now He'd shown Simon and
his fishing partners the whole truth. He could command
the seas, and its creatures responded to His word. He
could do things nobody else could do. He'd said so, and
now they'd seen it. The result?

Then they brought the boats to land, left
everything, and followed him. (v. 11)

"Everything." All their things.

They surrendered everything. All the fish they'd
been striving to catch, all the financial security their

hardworking enterprise had brought them, they left it all behind in an instant—even the largest single catch of fish they'd ever collected in their lives. Not because fish and fishing no longer mattered but because it no longer mattered *as much as* following Jesus, the One whose identity had become so strikingly clear to them.

An enormous catch had once been their highest aspiration, but now surrendering their all to Christ was the only thing they longed for. Because now they had no doubt about who He really was.

Over time, He would reveal even more about His identity to them, as well as to the crowd. And on that day when Jesus asked His disciples the piercing, poignant, powerfully personal question, "Who do you say that I am?" Peter could answer without reservation: "God's Messiah" (Luke 9:20). "You are the Messiah" (Mark 8:29). "You are the Messiah, the Son of the living God" (Matt. 16:16).

The roots of his confident declaration began on that morning when the coarsened ropes of Peter's fishing nets began coming apart under the weight of a miraculous catch. It started a process that would wreck and recalibrate his life, as well as those of all the others who were with him. It had shifted the trajectory of their goals and ambitions. It had changed the barometer they used for measuring success and failure.

Jesus had shown them who He really was, who He really is.

That's the making of a disciple.

❧

It is foundationally important, when thinking about discipleship and our willingness to surrender our all, to begin where Jesus did, by focusing on His identity. Not yours but His. Not your failings, weaknesses, and struggles but His fullness, perfection, and power. Because discipleship is costly. Incredibly costly. And let's not kid ourselves: we will not pay its price if we're not convinced to our core that the one we're serving with our all—with our everything—is totally worth it.

We can say we believe all the things the Scriptures say about Him, but if we really want to know how deep our belief in Him goes, our level of surrender will reveal the truth. We'll know it by how quickly and unreservedly we either leave the fish behind to become His followers or how tightly we grasp them. By how we surrender control to Him in the most treasured areas of our lives. To the extent that we trust His authority and character, that's the extent to which we'll be willing to align our whole lives to His leadership, even when what we're surrendering to Him feels countercultural or uncomfortable.

To demand this level of trust and commitment of us would be extortion if Jesus were anyone else. The only reason He can stake a claim to our *all* is because He was, and forever will be, the Son of God, for whom it was "necessary" to "suffer many things and be rejected by the elders" on His way to securing our salvation (Luke 9:22).

And because He is, and because He did, no other response should ever be expected from a disciple. No other response than this:

They "left everything" and "followed him."

The words Jesus used when describing the disciple's life are as clear and plain to us today as to those who heard Him speak it on that day.

> "If anyone wants to follow after me, let him
> deny himself, take up his cross daily, and
> follow me. For whoever wants to save his life
> will lose it, but whoever loses his life because
> of me will save it. For what does it benefit
> someone if he gains the whole world, and yet
> loses or forfeits himself?" (Luke 9:23–25)

Deny. Cross. Lose. Follow. These are sobering terms reminding us that being a disciple necessitates a solid divorce from much of what the society and even the Christian culture have purported and promoted. It flies in the face of a self-focused faith that celebrates excess, hustle, and a life of ease and comfort as the mark of God's favor on one's life. It reorients the compass of our religious activity back in the direction of simplicity, discipline, obedience, holiness, and the restraint His Spirit develops within us. It reminds us and requires of us a reckoning that leaves us with a sober-minded determination of purpose and with a definite choice to make.

Will we pursue this discipleship—Christ's definition of discipleship—or will we create our own definition that coddles our flesh and esteems this earth over the kingdom of heaven?

Consider His words again. Hear each progressive portion of His explanation of discipleship in terms of an answer to a question you or I might ask:

1. What is the essence of discipleship? "Deny yourself."
2. How do I accomplish this? "Take up your cross."
3. How often must I do this? "Daily."
4. Who is my model? "Me, follow Me."
5. What will the result be? "Lose your life for My sake, and you will find it."
6. Why is this important? "What do you profit by gaining the world but losing your soul?"

This is a scriptural pattern, the way Jesus presented this statement. He tells us to deny ourselves, take up our cross, and follow Him. Then He follows it up with clarifying sentiments on how to accomplish it.

By losing your life.

He is not referring to our physical life (although many martyrs have laid theirs down) but to our inner life as an individual, our self-life, the life we so easily devote to the earth's deluded offerings. We do it so naturally. We seek our security, significance, and identity in the things this world can only temporarily provide, wanting to "save" our lives, to "find" ourselves—something Jesus said He wants for us too—but we usually go about it the wrong way. The opposite way.

We obsessively pursue our personally defined goals and passions, looking to them as our gateway to approval, acceptance, and success. We strive to achieve the ambitious accolades we covet, the public admiration we desire, and the financial stability we believe will secure for us a settled and satisfying future. Nothing is inherently wrong with these things, unless and until we acquiesce our convictions to acquire them and then we attach our sense of identity to whether we receive them or not.

Here, though, is how we can usually tell our motives are off. We modify and manipulate our behaviors so that we're always tuning our conversations and determining our affiliations based on how well they help us reach these aspirations we've set for ourselves. We want to be the ones who end up "gaining the world," who end up winning at life.

But according to Christ's definition of discipleship, when these things are our primary pursuit, when we root our identity in them, they will be—even if we gain them—a greater threat to our fulfillment and purpose than we could ever imagine. Life, for the disciple, is only fulfilled when we intentionally choose a posture of self-denial, submission, and sacrifice to God.

Truly winning at life will require us "losing" our lives, detaching our sense of identity and significance away from the things of this world, attaching them instead to the identity of Christ.

We find ourselves by finding ourselves in Him. To seek fulfillment in any other way is to find ourselves empty in the end.

Earth's offerings can never be the ultimate, defining elements in the disciple's decision-making. It's not that they are negative, as if we must run from them and have nothing to do with them. The Lord, in His goodness and mercy, as a loving Father does, gives us many of the blessings that abound in this world for us to steward and enjoy. But too easily—oh, how easily—they can become a central, addictive focus until they've become an unspoken idol we orbit our lives around. When they're up and working for us, we're up too. When they're down and working against us, we're down too. They're always overwhelming us with the pressure to conform, and yet they leave behind so little for us to feel contented with.

So little to gain. So much to lose.

Let me ask you a little question here, which I'm asking of myself as well. It's simply a way of taking inventory, evaluating the amount of importance we're ascribing to things that are fighting against our disciple's heart. Think about the things you desire from this world. You know what they are. I know what mine are. How have you allowed them and the power they possess to shift your attitude, to control your time, to determine your moral compass, to provide the template for how you spend your day, to give your flesh more mastery over you than the life of Christ within? And, if the Spirit convicted you to leave one or more of them behind, would you? Could you? Surrender?

Wherever you notice an imbalance in the level of impact they have on you, recognize you've become *their* disciples instead of His. Yes, *their* disciples. Because we all are *someone's* disciples, *something's* disciples. And if we, wanting to be *Christ's* disciples, are not intentional about losing our lives to Him instead of losing to these competitors, resisting their seductive tie to our souls, we will always be pulled along by their enticing lure toward an unattainable finish line. Ultimately, they can offer us nothing but unfulfilled discouragement. But Jesus offers to us, His disciples, untold and eternal profit from our unfettered surrender.

‿͡ᴐ

"Who do the crowds say that I am?" (Luke 9:18). Someone worth respecting, someone worth observing, but just not someone worth following. The crowds never follow Christ—they can't follow Christ—because they don't really believe who He is.

But hear the Lord whisper the question to you today: "Who do you say that I am?"

That's the question the disciple must grapple with.

And this is the answer we must ultimately give: "There is one Lord, Jesus Christ. All things are through him, and we exist through him" (1 Cor. 8:6). The disciple finds her life in Him, in being "hidden with Christ in God" (Col. 3:3), so that everything of hers—every behavior, every word, every passion, every purpose—takes its surrendered place under the umbrella of imitating Christ and His example.

The boats and the nets are only worth leaving because the teacher—*this* Teacher—is worth following. Because this Teacher is not just a teacher. He is all. He is everything.

He is Jesus. The Christ. The Son of the living God.

Surrendering All

"Whoever does not bear his own cross and
come after me cannot be my disciple."
Luke 14:27

In what specific ways do you sense the Holy Spirit leading you to surrender and "deny yourself" in this season of
your life?

_____

_____

_____

_____

_____

_____

_____

_____

_____

_____

_____

_____

What does the level and promptness of your surrender
and obedience to Jesus reveal about your real view of His
identity and your commitment to Him?

_____

_____

_____

_____

_____

_____

_____

_____

_____

_____

_____

_____

_____

_____

Prayerfully consider what practical steps you can take to sever anything to which you've attached your significance and identity, so that you can tether it completely and wholly to Christ.

_____

_____

_____

_____

_____

_____

_____

_____

_____

_____

_____

_____

_____

_____

_____

_____

For Further Reading
John 8:31–32 • 2 Timothy 2:11 • Hebrews 10:21–22

CHAPTER 2

Everything You Need

"Remain in me, and I in you . . . because you
can do nothing without me."
John 15:4–5

The garage door wouldn't open.

There I sat, positioned behind the steering wheel, my purse in the seat next to me, my key in the ignition. I was ready to roll. And yet I couldn't go anywhere.

Because the garage door wouldn't open.

My husband came out and dragged his stepladder over to where the opener mechanism hung down from the ceiling. Then he proceeded to tinker and push around on things, as husbands are apt to do, trying to rouse it to action.

But nothing. And nowhere for me to go, not as long as that machine stayed unresponsive.

Thankfully, the manufacturer had put a sticker on the side which included a toll-free number to call for consultation and support if people who owned their product ever found themselves in a situation like this. Jerry called and attempted the few troubleshooting steps they recommended, making several adjustments to the unit. Still no good. Still no driving.

But maybe the problem lay somewhere else, the technician said. Maybe the issue wasn't with the settings inside the box at all, not with the motor or the chain or the harnesses or anything like that. Maybe it was something else altogether. Something really simple.

He then asked Jerry to turn his attention instead to the garage door itself, specifically to the little laser-beam devices that were anchored onto the bottom of the doorframes on each side, near the floor. If those little canisters had somehow gotten bumped or even slightly knocked out of place, there was a possibility the rays of light they emitted were no longer meeting each other's gaze the way they're designed to do. Because when those beams are aligned, when they're connected with each other, they communicate with the garage door opener and send out the signal that empowers the whole apparatus to work. As soon as Jerry checked their position—which, sure enough, was off by a small but significant enough degree—he was able to bend them back into agreement.

"Try to open it now," he said to me.

I punched the same button on the car remote that had produced nothing for me earlier, and—*whirr!*—the garage door opened up, and I was on my way.

Lack of alignment was the problem. Connection was the issue.

It was just one thing. So simple yet so critical to successful function.

True discipleship, the kind Jesus defined and described in Luke 9:23—where we deny ourselves, take up our cross, and follow Him—is impossible without one thing: being in right relationship with Him. Not just in a saved relationship with Him but in an ongoing, everyday, all-the-time *connection*—a relationship where His power is constantly flowing through us, enabling us to walk in holiness and victory.

The Scriptures describe the essence of this sacred alignment with one comprehensive word: *abide*. Against all our inclinations to work and to worry about whether our best efforts can ever measure up to the level of what His high calling demands, hear Jesus explain the most essential aspiration to us, just as He did to the eleven disciples mere hours before He would be crucified on Golgotha's tree:

"Abide in Me, and I in you." (John 15:4 NKJV)

In seven simple words, Jesus described the key for victorious, fruitful living and pinpointed the primary focus and pursuit of the disciple: *Abide in Me. Stay connected to Me. Focus on maintaining your alignment with Me.*

Our goal is to cultivate a deeper, richer, and more steadfast friendship with the Lord today than we had the day before, staying surrendered to Him, remaining obedient to Him. This is how the door to discipleship suddenly opens wide for us and the drive to follow Him is constantly inspired within us.

And then away we go. In ways we never thought possible.

∽

To underscore the importance of this message, let's open the Bible and hear Jesus speaking it to His disciples in its original, real-time context.

He was less than twenty-four hours from dying on the cross. And He knew it. He was even closer to that horribly fraught moment when He would be praying "drops of blood" to His Father in the garden of Gethsemane (Luke 22:44). The red-letter passages of John 14–17 were not His last words, but they were His final message to the close-knit group of Twelve (minus Judas) who'd been following Him for the past three years.

So although Jesus never did anything that wasn't 100 percent purposeful, you can be sure His intention behind *these* words, behind delivering *this* message to His closest companions at this critical juncture was especially significant. He wanted them ready for the challenging road they were soon to endure because of what He, their Lord, was soon to endure Himself.

They'd just finished sharing the Passover meal, somewhere in Jerusalem. After eating, He had unexpectedly wrapped a towel around His waist, brought over a basin of water, and washed their feet in an unforgettably stunning expression of His humility. He told them, even though He was going away, that He was "going to prepare a place" for them (John 14:2). And, despite His soon absence, He would not leave them here as "orphans" (v. 18), that He and His Father would send the Holy Spirit to them, to comfort and counsel them, to help keep them encouraged and anchored in truth, and to "remind" them of "everything I have told you" (v. 26).

Trouble was coming, yes. But they could always count on experiencing His "peace" (v. 27). He would never stop leading them and taking care of them, even from beyond the grave.

But He still had something more to tell them and to show them.

And so He instructed them to "get up; let's leave this place" (v. 31). He led them out of the city, through the winding streets of Jerusalem, across the Kidron Valley, and on toward the lower slopes of the Mount of Olives, in which the garden of Gethsemane was nestled, where the saga of His suffering would truly commence.

Along the way, before reaching the garden, they would've walked past local scenery that was as common to their daily experience as the dirt paths and flat-roofed homes that characterized their towns and villages. Here along the trails they'd so often traveled with Him, they would've passed by the familiar shapes and structures of working vineyards in full operation. Masterfully manicured. Meticulously maintained.

Seeing the tidy rows of grapes in full view surely induced within the disciples' souls a tangible feeling of happier times. In this era and culture, the plump fruit of the vineyard symbolized the sweetness of life, those festive seasons of the year when the entire community celebrated with laughter and rejoiced over the blessings of God on their harvests and in their lives. The presence of thriving clusters of grapes in the vineyards around town provided a visible confirmation of the good health they enjoyed as a people.

Good grapes meant good times.

Consider, then, the juxtaposition of this warm, satisfying sense of contentment alongside the looming heaviness and uncertainty that had been gathering around them all this unusual day and night. This stark contrast was an observation His disciples were sure to notice and to glean from this teachable moment. That's because the lesson He was about to share with them, here in the vineyard of John 15, was meant for disciples of every century yet to come, who would face their own inevitable periods of suffering, stress, and separation. And so, *before* the disciples reached Gethsemane, *before* they faced one of the darkest moments in their lives, Jesus taught them about the principle of abiding.

Lean in and listen, modern-day disciple.

In order to endure life's unavoidable trials and tribulations, we will need to learn and establish this same spiritual priority if we're going to be ready for what's coming. During those times when He allows us, by God's grace, to live in the relative ease of stability and normalcy—as the disciples felt when surrounded by the sweetness and goodness of grapes—it's imperative we use the opportunity to practice a particular spiritual habit that is essential to all those who want to remain steadfast in Christ.

Abide.

Because Gethsemane is coming.

Hard days will soon arrive, if they haven't already, when it'll be hard for us to think straight, days when we won't feel like we have enough resources available to us for surviving the pressures that are bearing down on us. But if we've been deliberate about homing in on this one foundational principle of discipleship as a top priority, He Himself will prepare us to stand strong through life's difficulties without wavering or walking away.

We'll be like Jesus, our Lord and Savior, who knew how to suffer because He knew where His strength came from.

There would be no grapes waiting for Him in Gethsemane. No good times. No fun and games. Yet He would be so *aligned* with His Father, so *connected* to the practice of doing His will, that He would be able to maintain a supernatural sense of stability amid the most unstable of circumstances.

The vineyard, Jesus said, has an *abiding* story to tell. And so, on the way to Gethsemane, He paused to offer the secret lesson learned from a vineyard full of grapes.

Abide.

Align.

Stay connected.

Begin to *Abide*

The Bible doesn't say, but I imagine Jesus stopping along their walk, motioning His disciples up close around Him to observe an important feature of the vineyard. Imagine the possibility that He leaned toward a particular vine He'd chosen for His classroom illustration. Picture Him running His hand along the thick, vibrant vine that grew up out of the ground, starting with the coarse, solid trunk at the base of the plant. Picture those hands that, as the Son of God, were almighty enough to hold the entire universe in their sustaining grip, yet, as man, could gently run their way up this single vine to the place where one of the fruit-bearing tendrils branched off from it.

See it with me, Him holding His hands right there—at this point of connection—between the vine and the branch.

Here was the natural juncture where life was organically transferred from base to branch, where an invisible source of energy deposited packets of nourishment from one place to the other, in ample portions.

"I am the vine; you are the branches." (John 15:5)

This is Me.
This is you.

Nature's art gallery paints this picture for us. Everything the branch needs for its survival and for its flourishing has its origin in that vine. *Everything.* Everything it needs. And as long as the branch stays connected to it, as long as the sinews within it continue to stay intermingled with the life that's flowing out of the vine, it lives. And it bears fruit. All the moisture and nutrients it requires just intrinsically make the journey from the starting point to the delivery point.

The life Jesus plans for us to get, He feeds it to us from Himself.

In other words, the branch doesn't need to strive and struggle to yield grapes on the back end because the vine is already supplying everything the branch needs on the front end. Our task as the branch in this simple illustration is merely to rest and receive—yes, to *rest* and *receive*—to draw from Him the spiritual strength that only the Vine, not we, can create. Our sole focus is to "remain" in Him, to abide in Him, to be aligned with Him—with His purposes, His ways, His character, His perspective through the regular rhythms of everyday life.

In nature, the branches simply *do* this. They stay put. Abiding is their only task. They don't struggle to keep connection or attempt to blossom any other way. They don't snap themselves off from the stem or the trunk to take their fruit-growing operation elsewhere, as if they don't really need this vine. But in your life and mine, we human branches tend to be less cooperative. We diminish the necessity of abiding for the sake of doing whatever gets us the most applause and admiration for our busyness and broad influence. We come up with our own plans and schedules, our own methods and formulas for performing at maximum productivity, and we strive and stress to bring them about. We fight our toughest temptations with buzzwords and brute force, in the name of achieving holiness. We live way out in the future, either worrying about what might happen or dreaming of what we hope to achieve, of the life we desire to have—this magical place where we'll be so happy and contented and fulfilled and masterful.

But all the striving is wasted exhaustion.

Because the connection itself is everything.

Don't read past this momentous teaching of Jesus, especially if you've heard it a thousand times, and think it's just a tad too simplistic for life in the real world. Nice in theory. Valuable in spots. Useful and usable in moderation. But *everything* can't be accomplished through *abiding*, Priscilla.

Yes, everything. Here, dear disciple, is everything you need. Everything you need comes from Christ. The branch, simply by resting and receiving, gets everything it needs.

∽

Notice there are three players on the stage of this word theater Jesus invited His disciples to attend. All three of the characters appear in the first five verses of John 15: (1) the "vine," (2) the "gardener," (3) the "branches."

> "I am the true vine, and my Father is the gardener. Every branch in me that does not produce fruit he removes, and he prunes every branch that produces fruit so that it will produce more fruit. You are already clean because of the word I have spoken to you. Remain in me, and I in you. Just as a branch is unable to produce fruit by itself unless it remains on the vine, neither can you unless you remain in me. I am the vine; you are the branches. The one who remains in me and I in him produces much fruit,

because you can do nothing without me."
(vv. 1–5)

Here's my question for you: Which ones of these three are seen as working? And which is described as resting and remaining?

- The vine is *working*—supplying life to the branches.
- The gardener is *working*—tending the garden, pruning and watering the plant, positioning the branches correctly to ensure they can produce maximum fruit.
- The branches are, what?—*not working*.

And yet flourishing. That's the point. That's our job—to remain connected and receive life, to submit ourselves to the Lord's wise and skillful methods for putting us in the best condition for bearing fruit, and then just growing there. That's it.

- The vine. *This is Me.*
- The gardener. *This is My Father.*
- The branches. *This is you. This is us.*

And to us, the Scripture says . . .

- "Stop striving and know that I am God."
  (Ps. 46:10 NASB)

- "Come to me, all of you who are weary
  and burdened, and I will give you rest."
  (Matt. 11:28)
- "His divine power has given us everything
  required for life and godliness." (2 Pet. 1:3)

Yes, it has. Let's stop acting as though these verses are not in the Bible or that God surely didn't mean them to be taken so literally like that. Yes, He did.

Resting and receiving.

Resisting all the striving and the struggling.

Or, as Jesus said to His main men on that intensely intimate night, . . .

> "You can do nothing without me." (John
> 15:5)

"Nothing" is what they could do. And "nothing" is what we can do, too, even in our pursuit of being His disciples.

The priority we're supposed to focus on is to remain, to abide, in the Vine.

The principle of abiding is such an important concept for us as disciples to understand and prioritize. John the apostle loved it so much that he included this word forty times in his Gospel and another twenty-seven times in his three letters: 1 John, 2 John, 3 John.

To "abide," as many of the older Bible translations interpret it, comes from the Greek word *meno*, meaning "to remain, to stay, to hang out with." It implies the sense of interconnectedness and alignment we've been talking about. It means to be immersed and enmeshed together.

To me, it means sipping a steamy cup of hot tea.

If you're someone who enjoys hot tea on occasion, you've maybe shared a table before with a friend or family member over a warm pot. I've noticed, as perhaps you have, there seem to be two types of tea drinkers. The first is what I'd call a *dipper*. She pours the boiling water over the tea bag into her cup, lets the bag rest there for a quick moment, then pinches the string between her fingers and repeatedly dips the tea bag in and out of the water, sometimes never stopping this dipping motion the whole time she's drinking, as if she's afraid to leave it submerged too long. A matter of taste, you say. Yes, I agree. If someone doesn't like her tea too strong, that's a good way to keep it from becoming overpowering, too intense for her liking.

But then there's the *abider*. The one who just leaves the tea bag there. She lets it soak. She lets it simmer without interruption. She lets all the deep, soothing flavors of the tea bag infuse every liquid molecule inside that cup.

I'm not telling you how to drink your tea. That's up to you. I'm just saying, if you and I want to experience the strength of God changing our behavior, changing our reactions, changing our desires, changing our whole lives, you can't dip in on Sundays and then dip out on Mondays. You can't dip in when life is hard and then dip out when things are stable and steady. No, the tea bag has to stay in the cup without interruption. Fully immersed, fully abiding. Tuesday at 2:00 looks the same as Sunday at 10:00. So does Friday at midnight. Weeknights and weekends. We are always considering Him, pursuing Him, talking with Him, trusting Him, obeying Him, checking to be sure we are in alignment with Him.

Here's what abiding looks like: being alert to His presence and His purposes while always resting, always receiving, yet amazingly becoming more fruitful than ever.

In what areas of your life are you striving right now? I don't mean a healthy productivity and commitment to what God has called you to do, whether at home or in business or at the studio or in ministry. As we'll talk about in the next several chapters, a lifestyle of abiding is not a license to laziness. I'm talking about those areas in your life where you're currently pressing way beyond the point of godly diligence, toward a ruthlessly overindulgent ambition. Your leading emotion is frustration. You sometimes think you're hurtling toward a state of emotional, spiritual, or physical collapse because you're trying to do so much, feeling like the upkeep of the world is resting squarely on your shoulders. To add to the pressure, you hope to impress other people, wanting to receive their applause.

Perhaps you've also slipped back into seeking out some of your old escapes, those addictive ties to certain pleasures that draw you into their seductive web, enticements that seem to know when you're dying for something to deaden the pain and the panic you sometimes feel. You've sacrificed your family and other relationships. You've lost sight of some of the disciplines and convictions that used to be high priorities. You've even forfeited your own needs, your own health, in this wild pursuit of what only the Vine can give you anyway.

Trust me on this. The way to start again is to trust that He is able to nourish and sustain you.

To surrender your striving. All of it.

To rest in Him. To receive from Him. To focus on cultivating a deeper connection with Him.

To abide in Him.

Choose Authenticity

Many Christmases ago, when one of our sons was fairly little, we gave him one of those remote-controlled vehicles that were so popular at the time. The one he'd wanted was a helicopter that, as toys go, was surprisingly big, heavy, and lifelike. On the box, and in his mind, were images of a sleek, gleaming helicopter flying high above the house and way out across the yard, for hours on end, performing acrobatic dips and spectacular landings.

There was a bit of a disconnect, however, between the product as advertised and the experience of it in reality. We soon learned that powering up the batteries required four hours of charging time. And even after keeping it plugged in for that long, completely out of commission, the total amount of flying time was only fifteen minutes per charge. Santa had been a little disappointing on this one.

And our son wasn't pleased.

Four hours felt like forever to a little boy eager to pilot his new flying machine. So we started to observe that after he would grow impatient for the lights on the instrument panel to burn a solid green, he would *pretend* he'd kept it charging for the whole allotted time. He even went so far as to grab one of our watches and move the hands forward four hours on the clock in an effort to convince himself that he'd done what he was supposed to do. Then he'd snatch up the control module, expecting to have a good long play with his new toy. But the actual flying time told us (and him) the truth. The chopper was not fully charged. When it was out of juice, it was out of juice, whether he wanted it to be or not.

There simply aren't shortcuts for certain things. The same is true in our spiritual lives. You can't skip the charging time and expect to get the full results. No matter how successfully you may fool others with all the external markings of someone who's cultivated a friendship in Christ or how diligently you even attempt to fool *yourself* into skipping the private, personal disciplines that infuse you with spiritual strength, the veneer, sooner or later (usually sooner) won't be able to mask the deficiency. You'll run out of gas trying to keep yourself moving.

There is nothing—no activity, no good deeds, no ministry work, no platform, no measure of influence—that can take the place of abiding. Of having a rich prayer life. Of listening and being sensitive to the leading of the Spirit. Of leaning into the Scriptures to understand the heartbeat of your Lord. Of being obedient to His directives. As disciples, this is the one thing we just cannot undercut. If we are inconsistent and impatient, constantly trying to outrun or avoid this critical spiritual virtue, we'll be running on fumes; and, more importantly, we will not produce any eternal fruit.

∽

In the vineyard of Christian living, it is possible for a branch to look connected without *being* connected. It can have a cosmetic connection to the vine—skin to skin touchpoints—but not really share in the life source that's intended to flow into each branch from Christ. Any branch that is superficially joined to Him, or is only sporadically joined to Him, will not produce fruit in any abundant measure. But "those who remain in me, and I in them," Jesus said, "will produce *much* fruit" (John 15:5 NLT, emphasis added).

Authentic abiding is the difference.

In other words, abiding cannot be achieved through surface connection. Abiding isn't decorative. A branch that is disconnected internally from the veins, from the real moisture and sinew of the vine will soon bear no more than the showy leaves and blossoms of a believer whose attachment is only skin-deep. It *looks* nice. It *dresses* nice. It may conform to a lot of the characteristics that today's Christian culture equates to Christian success. But push away the flowery curb appeal, and where's the fruit?

This is why we must be so careful, friend, to stay authentically connected with Him. To truly surrender all. To pursue Him privately in prayer, in the study of His Word, and in keeping our ear tuned to the Spirit's conviction far more than we seek to perform in the public eye. It is possible to work hard for Him but not be connected to Him. It is possible to check off the to-do list of religious activity, to attend church, to participate in (or even lead) a weekly Bible study meeting but not be aligned with Him. To others, it can look like you have an abiding, meaningful, ongoing friendship with Jesus. Sure seems like it. Sure sounds like it. But underneath, the connection is shallow. The reason you're not feeling His nourishment deep down is because you only plug into Him when you need to be *ON*, not during those off times when you're off duty, when you're offline, and seeking your charge from any other vines than the "true vine" (John 15:1).

When people tell me they're struggling spiritually, feeling stagnant (or when I'm feeling that way myself), one of the ways I often point them toward this principle of abiding is by asking probing questions like these:

- Are your public ministry activities outpacing the private spiritual disciplines that create a friendship with Jesus?
- Do you feel frenzied with activity *for* Jesus without sensing a fervent and authentic friendship *with* Jesus?

If the answer to either or both of these questions is *maybe* or *yes* (which has been *my* true answer at different seasons of life), resist the urge to add anything else to your list of religious activities, even good things like going into another group Bible study series. Instead, rest where you are. Relearn, absorb, and incorporate into your life the truths He taught you from the *last* Bible study you did. Abide *there*. Remain prayerful *there*. Talk to the Lord about where you are, and ask Him what He wants to do in your life now to reorient yourself to the lessons He has already revealed to you. Allow time for the deep work of the Holy Spirit to strengthen and sustain you there. Cultivate a friendship with Jesus *right there*.

Many genuine believers would always rather do something, achieve something, or accomplish something because this surface-layer stuff feels more like making progress. At least that's what the bent of Christianity in the Western world has erroneously led us to believe. The more we do, the more expansive our platform becomes, the more industrious we appear to be, then the more celebrated we are. So give us a new Bible study book to complete, sign us up for a mission trip to take, register us for another conference to attend, or give us another ministry to undergird or a platform to expand, and it looks like we're growing. People think we're flourishing in our relationship with Jesus.

But the authentic life of Christ that we need comes to us typically in less visible ways, in under-the-surface ways, down where human eyes can't see, where roots run deep, in private where we abide with Him. And because this part of the process is happening under the surface, like the life of a grapevine does, our tendency (and the tendency of those watching us from afar) is to devalue this authentic flow of life. That's the reason we feel so tempted to replace it, to replace Him, with something else, with something more visible, with something more tangible, with something that gives us the false, yet refreshing sense that we're doing something "fruitful."

But it will be fake fruit if we're faking at being His branches.

Receive Assurance

Jesus, remember, was on His way to Gethsemane when He taught the disciples this lesson about grapes, vines, branches, and abiding. Shortly after His arrival in the garden, one of His closest friends—one of the disciples who rightly should've been here in John 15 with all the others—would reveal himself as Christ's betrayer.

Life on earth can be like that. It is set up to betray us. Our body, over time, will fail us. Our friends will disappoint us. Our spouse, even if not betraying us, will still prove less than the "everything" we thought him to be when we married him. (We wives, to be fair, prove no more reliable.) Our children will upset us. Our house and our car will break down on us. Technology will malfunction at a critical moment. The government will make promises it can't fulfill. We are simply surrounded by people, places, and things that are so often less than the sum of our expectations. And one of those people was the person we saw in our bathroom mirror last night.

But Jesus, He said, will never leave us or forsake us. The reason we can afford to "remain" in Him is because He has promised to remain in us. And not just *remain* in us but keep empowering us, keep supplying life to us, keep investing in us, keep working inside us.

That's the assurance we can experience from being connected to "the true vine" (John 15:1 NASB). He will not betray us. His life will never disappoint us. He will not let us down or fail to be present at the times we need Him most. If it rains, the vine is there. If it hails, the vine is there. Day and night, winter and summer, the vine is our constant connection to spiritual food and solid ground.

And the same assurance we derive from being connected to the vine, we also receive from being cared for by the vinedresser.

The purpose of the "gardener" (the vinedresser) in Jesus's roadside illustration, as well as in our right-now reality, is to coax as much fruit as possible from His beloved vineyard. He views each branch under His watchful care with an eye toward helping us bring forth the maximum amount of fruit that He created us to produce.

The branches on a hearty grapevine, at any point in time, can still experience challenges. Other forces are weighing on them or encroaching on them, which can impair their ability to receive what they need for growth. Knocked over by strong wind, some of the branches can end up trailing along the ground, where they easily become weighed down in the dirt and mud, coated with external debris or at risk of being trampled. Some branches find themselves tangled within thickets of other branches, which block the sunshine from reaching them, overcrowding their space, and preventing them from producing up to their full capability.

And so God our Father, in the vineyard His disciples dwell in, does for us what the seasoned, experienced vinedresser does among the grapevines—with gloves on, in work boots, with sharpened gardening tools in hand.

When we've fallen into the mud of sin and rebellion, the Lord reaches down and lifts us up. He cleans off the grime we've collected from being down at the bottom, and—like a vinedresser who repositions the branches, securing them to a nearby trellis—our Father turns our faces back toward the light, to live another new day under the banner of His grace and goodness.

Be reassured, my fellow branch. He will not leave us down there, down in the thick of our worst moments. "If we confess our sins, he is faithful and righteous to forgive us our sins and to cleanse us from all unrighteousness" (1 John 1:9). We can't flourish in the dirt. We weren't made for the raggedy living conditions in the slop where we sometimes seek to go and to stay. It won't be easy coming up. It'll stretch us in ways that our wills have not been accustomed to bending. But the discipline and correction of the vinedresser, though uncomfortable, are conducted with our best in mind. He works hard to liberate us from sin and to reposition us for better growth.

But He also does something else. Something more.

He prunes us to stop the growth we only *think* is growth.

Because it is possible for a branch to be flowering prolifically, so that to the untrained eye it seems to be the healthiest of the bunch. But the wise gardener knows this profusion of foliage can actually work against the branch's true potential. The sprouting of impressive blooms is not the Gardener's goal for His branches. He's after grapes.

This sobering reality bears repeating. It is possible for us to be flowering but not fruitful. We can be impressive but not producing. We can be a darling of devotion to Him on social media but not be honoring to Him in our hearts. We can appear to have all the sparkle of spiritual success yet be choking on our own proud reputation.

But be reassured, my fellow branch. He loves you too much to let you have the appearance of fruitfulness without the reality of it.

So the clippers must come out—to prune away unnecessary things, which can even be good things, but they're weighing you down and entangling you from bearing the fruit He had in mind when He planted you.

We once lived on a country road that was lined on either side by tall, thick pockets of greenery. It felt refreshing to drive through it. Full branches of leaves shimmering in the breezy sunshine. A lush canopy of trees overhead. Little dots of wildflowers chasing up along the trunks, adding scents of color to the country drive.

Then one day, as I was heading home down our beautiful little two-lane paradise, I came almost to a stop in the road. The mowers had been there, and they'd left behind their bite marks. Mounds of limp branches, twigs, and leaves lay in heavy piles along both ditches. The trees now looked mutilated, their wooden shards of sheared-off branches sticking out at harsh, spiky angles. Where beauty had once been all you could see, now you could see right through them. And it wasn't pretty. It didn't seem fair.

Some of the neighbors called the county office. How could they have allowed this to happen? Why would they come and deface our street like this? What would become of all the shade and ambience that had taken all this time to grow up and develop?

But the wiser, more tenured neighbors knew better, as did the agricultural advisors who'd sent the men out to work on this project. "Give it six months," one of our nearby friends said to us as we were bemoaning the loss of what we'd come to love, "and it'll come back better than ever. The pruning makes it possible."

The vinedresser is not only a planter; He's also a pruner. He "prunes every branch," for the purpose of making each one "produce more fruit" (John 15:2). So His pruning is not a problem; it's a promise. It's for our good. It's for our growth.

A good friend may relocate and move to another place, but God is only pruning us through this loss to produce more fruit. Our job may be eliminated, our application may be denied, but our God is only cutting something away from us to encourage new growth in us. An opportunity we'd long desired may be slipping right through our fingers, but our Father, the vinedresser, is only allowing what the best and wisest gardeners do. He is trimming us back, down to the nub if necessary, in full anticipation of a fuller season of productivity and fruitfulness.

It can feel like rough, raw, unreasonable restriction. But to the one who's surrendered her all to Him, even the pruning can be received as loving reassurance—the assurance that He has not stopped working to fulfill His purpose in her. In us.

Experience Abundance

The older I get, the less easily impressed I become by people. I'm not impressed by flash. I'm not impressed by sheer talent. I'm not impressed by what's popular and making headlines. None of that. I'm mostly just impressed now by people who are faithfully bearing fruit.

Not fame, fruit.

Not fortune, fruit.

Not followers, fruit.

Not friends, fruit.

"You did not choose me," Jesus said to His disciples, "but I chose you," and . . .

> "I appointed you to go and produce fruit, and that your fruit should remain, so that whatever you ask the Father in my name, he will give you." (John 15:16)

Fruit. What is this "fruit" He's talking about?

The fruit the vine produces through us are thoughts, attitudes, and actions that glorify God. Good works we do that bless others and draw attention to Him. They grow within us internally, the fruit of the Spirit: "love, joy, peace, patience, kindness, goodness, faithfulness, gentleness, and self-control" (Gal. 5:22–23).

- Instead of being selfish, we're servant hearted, like Jesus is.
- Instead of being cowardly, we're courageous, like Jesus is.
- Instead of being anxious, we're restful, relaxed, and patient, like Jesus is.
- Instead of being bitter, we're understanding and forgiving, like Jesus is.

Christ's heart and humility, shining through us.

But that's not all, because His fruit can't stay contained inside. "Every good tree produces good fruit,"

Jesus said (Matt. 7:17). The changes happening within us eventually become lasting changes happening on the outside of us, in visible ways, in noticeable ways, in ways that identify us as genuine followers of Jesus and have eternal value. "So that they may see your good works and give glory to your Father in heaven" (Matt. 5:16). "My Father is glorified by this: that you produce much fruit and prove to be my disciples" (John 15:8).

This, my friend, is the abundant life. Not things. Not money. Not clicks. Not comforts. The purpose behind God's transfer of life and power to us—from the Father, through the Son, and by the presence of the Holy Spirit— is to enable our fully surrendered lives to produce fruit of eternal value. Not to achieve temporal success but to bear long-lasting, year-over-year production. Not to look good for the cameras but to look like Jesus to the world.

It's worth the complete surrender because it completes His and our every joy.

Disciples don't work at being disciples. They surrender their striving, and then they abide in Christ. They *rest* and *receive* from the real, authentic vine, find their *reassurance* in His presence, and yield a *rich*, eternal harvest from His life.

Surrendering All

My heart has heard you say, "Come and talk with me."
And my heart responds, "LORD, I am coming."
Psalm 27:8 NLT

Looking back over your life, what activities, good deeds, ministry work, platforms, or other measures of influence have you let override your priority on abiding with Jesus?

_____

_____

_____

_____

_____

_____

_____

_____

_____

_____

If you've felt a dullness in your spiritual life, prayerfully consider your response to the following questions from this chapter:

- Are your public ministry activities outpacing the private spiritual disciplines that create a friendship with Jesus?
- Do you feel frenzied with activity *for* Jesus without sensing a fervent and authentic friendship *with* Jesus?

Discuss with someone the principle of abiding, someone whose depth of relationship with the Lord you admire. What are the priorities and rhythms of their spiritual growth that you can adopt?

_____

_____

_____

_____

_____

_____

_____

_____

_____

_____

_____

_____

_____

For Further Reading
Psalm 63:1 • Psalm 105:4 • 1 John 2:6

CHAPTER 3

Everything You Are

To all who did receive him, he gave them the right to be children of God, to those who believe in his name.
John 1:12

March 9, 1974, a fifty-one-year-old lieutenant of the Japanese army emerged from a jungle hideout on the tiny Philippine island of Lubang.[1] Those who encountered him were shocked. His uniform was tattered and ill-worn, hanging bulkily around his slender frame. His belt contained a number of outdated analog gadgets and instruments, useful for survival and subterfuge. The handle of a pistol was visible at his waist. A samurai sword dangled dangerously at his left side.

He'd obviously been engaged in battle of some sort or was at least still capable of it. He was certainly still prepared for it. He looked the part of a soldier. Yet he appeared to be a warrior from another time, from an era that no longer existed.

The last known sighting of him had been during World War II, in 1944—thirty years earlier—when he was dispatched to defend the remote airstrip on this island from being used by enemy planes. And though the Japanese had surrendered soon after he began his clandestine work, the news never officially reached him. He never knew to abandon his mission.

Even as airdropped leaflets floated down from U.S. planes, informing any remaining soldiers that the war was over, he didn't believe it. He *couldn't* believe it. According to the code of battle that had been baked into him during combat training, the identity of a soldier was fixed and unchangeable. He'd been told that the soldier never gave up. The soldier was never taken prisoner. The soldier didn't surrender. The soldier died fighting, or he fought on forever.

In his mind, his old identity was his only identity.

And so, for far too many additional years, he stayed locked into performing the duties that corresponded with his original assignment, living off the land in poverty, stealing food from area farmers to survive, and readying himself for a battle that he'd long been released from fighting.

Not until his now-retired superior officer journeyed from Japan to the Philippines and formally discharged him from his archaic orders did the old soldier agree to relent, lay down his arms, come home from his jungle existence, and step out of character as a World War II soldier. Only then did he stop fighting a battle that had already ended years ago.

Only then would he consider assuming . . .

A new identity.

༒

Consider this chapter your new marching orders, fellow soldier. Hear your Superior Officer command you to lay down the accoutrements that may have served you in a previous era but do not serve you now. The way of living that may have worked for you in your previous existence no longer aligns with this new one you've been called to enjoy. Assume the new identity that is rightfully yours. It's time. Stop acting like you are still in a battle that's already been won. Take off the old war clothes that don't fit the freedom and abundance you are called to exist in now. Stop living below your spiritual means, scraping by, hiding out, and operating in fear. That's not who you are.

Not anymore.

Not here.

Not now.

Not ever.

You have a new identity.

Discipleship, at its core, is a question of *identity*. Mistaken identity. Misplaced identity. Whenever we sense a lack of willingness to surrender all, our problem usually centers around our misunderstanding of who we truly are now as victors in Christ.

Because if we knew now what He has saved us to be—
if we truly believed what His Word tells us about who
we are now—we'd surrender all and call off this fight.
We'd go where the truth is leading us. We'd be convinced
there's nothing to gain by trying to hold on to what we've
previously known or to the lifestyle assumptions we've
always had. We'd surrender our all to Him because we'd
know our identity is secure in Him, and we'd change our
entire lifestyle to line up with our *new* identity.

When you became a believer, a shift took place in
your identity, both immediately and necessarily. You were
given the gift of a new nature. Your old nature died, the
one that was contaminated by sin and forced to follow its
demands, the one that was captured by sin's unholy lusts,
unable to walk in freedom and fullness.

This "old self" of yours was "crucified" with Christ,
"so that the body ruled by sin might be rendered power-
less," so that you would "no longer be enslaved to sin"
(Rom. 6:6). The finished work of Jesus on the cross finished the hold of sin over your life. Instead of being governed by it any longer, and instead of being bossed around
by every whim and impulse of the devil, you received the
Holy Spirit's empowerment in order to shift the kinds of
choices you were able to make. Instead of being equipped
for serving sin, you were equipped for serving God, for
honoring Him with your life, for living with the purpose
of putting Him first in everything.

Many believers do not grow any further in their faith simply because they're unaware of this foundational identity shift.

They still think the original, sin-sick version of themselves is their current one. Based on their past, they don't feel like they have any choice but to follow its foolish lead. Either because they haven't been told or they've just not been able to wrap their heads around this life-transforming change, they do not fully understand that their former identity is not their present identity, that God has "rescued" them from the "domain of darkness," that He has "transferred" them into the "kingdom of the Son he loves" (Col. 1:13), that "the old has passed away, and see, the new has come" (2 Cor. 5:17). They, and we, are now *dead to sin*.

AND . . .

We are *alive to God*. Dead to what kills us, alive to what saves us. Just as Christ was not only crucified but was also resurrected, we too have experienced not only the death of our old self but also the resurrection of our new self. Though we were once "dead in [our] trespasses," God has "made us alive with Christ." He has "raised us up with him and seated us with him in the heavens in Christ Jesus" (Eph. 2:5–6). It's a magnificent identity shift for the ages.

The reason our redemption story doesn't stop at the cross is because death is not the end of it. Being dead to sin is merely our starting point. Our new, resurrected identity amazingly situates us in heavenly places with Christ and seats us in a position of eternal victory, where by His Spirit we can hear from God, please God, pursue God, and have our thinking transformed by the mind of God. This is not somebody else we're talking about. This is you. This is who you are.

Dead to sin, fully alive to God.

Paul said it the following way in another of his New Testament letters, as if he was working to grapple with the wonder of it himself, with the majestic mystery of what Jesus had done for him:

> I have been crucified with Christ, and I no
> longer live, but Christ lives in me. The life
> I now live in the body, I live by faith in the
> Son of God, who loved me and gave himself
> for me. (Gal. 2:20)

"So, you too," he said, "consider yourselves dead to sin and alive to God in Christ Jesus" (Rom. 6:11). This statement of your identity—as someone "dead to sin" and "alive to God"—forms the real and rational basis for your discipleship and your fully surrendered life in Christ.

But will you believe it when you hear it?

And will you keep believing it when you doubt it?

〜

The first chapter of Ephesians provides the most con-centrated place in Scripture for us to view our Christian identity in one place. I encourage you, if you can't do it right now, make time to read it real soon. And then read it over again. And again. Meditate on it. Savor the words and phrases of it. Wrap your heart and mind around it. (Also, quote it to your children and grandchildren so their own lives can be shaped by it too.)

Sometime in the next twenty-four hours, allow Ephesians 1 to impact every aspect of how you think about yourself as a believer in Christ. That'll be time well spent.

When you do, here are a few other things you'll dis-cover about who you are in Christ:

You've been chosen. "For he chose us in him, before the foundation of the world, to be holy and blameless in love before him" (v. 4). He didn't just choose us to change us; He chose us to accept us. That's what the "holy and blameless" part is all about. I mean, we know better than anyone how far our lives have been from "holy and blame-less." Yet God in His love and mercy is justified in consid-ering us pure because we've received the life of Jesus inside us. We are "holy and blameless" to Him because He sees in us the "holy and blameless" purity of His Son's sacrifice for us. And because of this, we are acceptable to Him.

The Bible says God cannot dwell with sin (see Ps. 5:4; Hab. 1:13), but He can accept things that are holy. And we are holy, you and I, because He has chosen to make us holy and blameless before Him. This is who you are.

You are forgiven. "In him we have redemption through his blood, the forgiveness of our trespasses, according to the riches of his grace" (Eph. 1:7). You are free from condemnation. Acquitted in His heavenly courtroom. You are released to live and operate within the wide blue ocean of His grace rather than the tight, demanding confines of guilt and shame.

You are an heir. You've inherited a tremendous treasure, "the wealth of his glorious inheritance in the saints" (v. 18). You may not be rich by the financial standards of today's world, but your divine Benefactor has promised you a robust spiritual endowment, more lavish and lasting than any portfolio or possessions known to man. Much of your inheritance is awaiting you in your eternal dwelling place with God, but even the first tastes of it—including the "promised Holy Spirit" who came to live in you "when you believed" (v. 13)—are beyond all the blessings we could dare to deserve. Your Giver delights in giving to you because of who you are to Him.

So now, consider the life-transforming potential for any of us who will choose to surrender ourselves to this new identity, to live in light of just these three components of it.

Think of it: you, accepted and chosen, handpicked by God, no longer needing to prove yourself to others or procure their acceptance, knowing you're already accepted by the only one whose opinion of you actually matters. How would this awareness, if you could believe it, impact how you choose to respond on your social media feeds or whether you choose to respond at all? How would it help you determine where you invest the bulk of your time and energy—whether to agree to a particular opportunity or project, whether to accept an invitation or decline with confidence? Would it quiet the anxiety bubbling up within your soul when you feel excluded by others or how you respond when you've been overlooked or misunderstood?

What about being *forgiven*? Perhaps you're someone who almost naturally shrinks back in shame, someone who makes many of her decisions from a defeated posture of guilt and self-reproach. How would these tendencies change as a person God has forever forgiven? What could you do now when those old feelings invade your heart, when you feel crippled by regret, when you're afraid to return to Him because you've lost ground to another failure and are tempted to feel like you're such a huge disappointment to Him? If you knew you were forgiven—if you realized "forgiven" is descriptive of your right-now identity—wouldn't you be more clearheaded when making decisions about your life? Lighter and more liberated?

You'd breathe easier, and you'd no longer allow past mistakes to dictate the outcome of your current reality and future.

And as an *heir* of great spiritual wealth—of "every spiritual blessing in the heavens in Christ" (v. 3)—would you continue to scrape the barrel for leftovers in your friendships or your romantic relationships? Or would you choose to be part of endeavors and interactions that befit a person whose Father deems her of endless value to Him? Wouldn't it change the way you approach situations and other encounters where you've routinely felt outmatched or underresourced? Instead of functioning from a stance of scarcity and lack, couldn't you afford to serve and to sacrifice, to be joyfully openhanded, knowing your inheritance can never be diminished by pouring out its blessings on others?

Because of who you are. Because of your new identity.

It's how surrendering *all* can finally make sense.

Because you're gaining more than you're releasing.

. ᴄᴏ

If you're looking for a single visual to help you capture your identity in Christ, Ephesians 1 delivers a most appropriate image: *adoption*.

My cousin Anne fostered a beautiful baby girl for three years. During that time, they developed a sweet bond that knitted their hearts together in an indelible way. And yet parental and family rights, rightly so, are strongly protected in our system of law. So any action taken by a foster parent to officialize her relationship with a child she's grown to love and care for, even when it's clear that her biological parents will not be responsible, is an arduous, slow-moving undertaking. You don't seek to legally adopt without determining in your heart to do it and being willing to wait a long time for the object of your love to become yours.

In this case, even if not in all cases, every possible avenue was taken to restore the child's relationships with her relatives, but they remained uncommitted and uncooperative. Their interest in the child was easy to question, given the promises they rarely kept and the emotional aggravation they added to an already tense and difficult situation. But despite the validity of the arguments Anne made as to why her home offered a more stable, suitable environment for this little girl to grow up and thrive in, the issue remained in doubt for what seemed like forever.

Nearly three years and thousands of tears later, including dozens of sleepless nights and an endless cycle of mediations and court cases, Marie finally became Anne's legal daughter. And at the instant when the judge pounded the gavel and declared the adoption final, this little girl's entire identity shifted.

She had a new last name and a new place to call home. She had a new parent and a new future, along with all the rights and privileges that went along with being part of her new family.

And listen to this: the access her previous family once maintained in relationship to her was legally terminated. They no longer had *the right* to interact with her as they pleased. They could not require anything of her or make decisions for her life. As a result of this new, official, court-ordered dynamic, their restrictive tie to her was severed.

The old was gone; the new had come.

And let me tell you, dear child of God, this adoptive change of identity is what the Lord has done for you and me too.

> He predestined us to be adopted as sons
> through Jesus Christ for himself, according
> to the good pleasure of his will, to the praise
> of his glorious grace that he lavished on us in
> the Beloved One. (Eph. 1:5–6)

You've been adopted into a new family. By virtue of this rebirth, you now have access to all the blessings your new Father delights to bestow on you. You don't need to earn them; you don't need to behave a certain way to keep them. They are yours. Your identity will always be yours because you are a daughter whose Father sought you out, chose you, grafted you into His care, loves you fiercely, and always makes good on His promises.

But your adoption also means something else. As surely as God has given you something new, He's taken something old away. The unhindered access your enemy once used to harm you, mistreat you, and keep you subject to his designs and influence is now entirely over. He is legally bound from governing you, now that God your Father has claimed you. He will try to interfere with you and look for ways to lure your affections back to him. He will drop false hints suggesting he still has the power to force you into doing what he says. But hear me clearly: he does not. His day is done. He can come around looking for you, but you can call the Authority on him if he does.

You are free to move about the cabin, my fellow disciple. Free to live in a home where you are safe. Free to live in a relationship where you are loved. And that means you are free to live in a family of followers where the practice of surrendered discipleship is the new normal.

But to experience it, you've got to believe it. Believe now in who you are, just as His Word says of you. Part of your privilege as an adopted daughter of your heavenly Father is to absorb and incorporate this new spiritual identity so completely into your soul that it infiltrates all your daily living. Throughout your lifetime, from one season and year to the next—from grace to grace and from glory to glory—keep renewing your mind to grasp the extent of what it truly means to be *His* adopted child.

Get accustomed to being called by a new name, to being known as His beloved.

Begin shifting to a new family dynamic, one in which your Father is faithful and true, His home is yours and is open to you, and His loving mercy says there is always hope of restoration, even after a fall.

Start living in light of your new family's resources instead of thinking of yourself as inferior and impoverished, instead of feeling the incessant need to come out on top in all those silly contests of comparison we play with others.

You're somebody new.

Believe it and get out there and live like it. Reframe and cement your new identity in your mind because it will enable you to walk in victory as a true disciple.

What a shame it would be if, as she matured, Marie never exercised the rights that were now hers to enjoy. What if she chose instead to remain stuck in the idea that she had no choice but to become a product of all the dysfunction connected to her previous situation and was unable to shake free of it or expect any other life than the one it offered? But this is what so many Christians do.

Maybe they attend church and wear religious paraphernalia, but they still think the old version of themselves is the more accurate description of their identity.

Maybe they regularly post faith-based comments on social media, but inside they feel tethered to a life where saying no to temptation is something they can't imagine actually being able to sustain, and where surrendering themselves fully to Christ is not really a workable possibility.

Maybe they read their Bible occasionally to check it off their obligatory to-do list, but the frame of mind they carry around with them has never shifted to align with what the Scripture says about their new standing in Christ. They still operate as if the lusts of their flesh are the captain of their lives, instead of realizing these tyrants have no power anymore over someone who is *dead to sin and alive to God.*

We have such a hard time believing it, don't we? Despite the showers of messages coming down from the pulpit at church and from the pages of Scripture at home, telling us we should feel so assured and victorious, that we are heirs to so much abundance, many believers blow these off as being no more than spiritual well-wishes. But if we'll choose to *abide* in Jesus, if we'll choose to believe what God says about our *identity* in Him, and then make our decisions, choose our behaviors, and shift our perspectives to align with it, this war we keep fighting inside can at last become a surrender we can finally live with.

Christ has already done the impossibly hard part to make this identity a reality for us. He died for us in order to adopt us. All we need to do now is cooperate with Him so He can grow in us a disciple's heart, the kind of heart that bears the fruit He has saved us to produce.

⌒⌒

During the COVID shutdown of 2020, I did a lot of things I hadn't made time for doing before. One of the hobbies I adopted was gardening. Now, just to be clear, I don't have a green thumb. None of my other fingers are green either, not even my pinkie. Still, I was eager to try my hand at it, but I knew I needed to keep it as simple as possible.

So instead of doing it the old-fashioned way by going out and digging up the backyard, I ordered one of those indoor, hydroponic gardening systems that provides you everything you need for the whole operation. I didn't want to be left to the mercy of the scorching Texas sun or the occasional summer shower.

This self-contained gardening tower, according to the advertising copy, would allow me to grow fruits and vegetables right there inside my quarantine house. It works by using ring lights, set to timers that switch on and off at precision intervals, as well as a water pump that pushes hydration into the soil. Sounded like a wonderful, low-maintenance plan for a wary, low-confidence gardener.

Several days after placing my online order, an enormous package arrived on my front porch, containing all the parts necessary for me to start my garden: the tower, the water pump, the ring lights, the timers, the seeds, the soil, plus some additional nutrients and vitamins. Everything in one box. Once I got all the equipment together and synchronized the timer for the lights and the water, the last piece of business was to plant the little seeds. That's because all the fancy, newfangled gardening stuff in the world can't produce anything to eat without including God's basic food-building block.

Seeds.

They're pretty amazing, really, when you think about them. The seeds that came in my packet already possessed everything inside them to produce what they were created for. Everything that was required for them to become a plant, which would then become a homegrown side item for me to put on my family's dinner table at night, was already tucked inside each of their sturdy little shells.

Those seeds contained everything inside them already for growing up into what the instruction manual said they could become. Infusing them with that potential is God's job. Only He can do that. But I needed to be responsible for planting them in suitable containers. And once they were planted, if I wanted them to grow healthfully, I needed to be diligent and disciplined in feeding them the weekly nutrition prescribed for helping them flourish and blossom.

Because, what good is having a seed I'm not willing to cultivate?

Let's connect this analogy now to the lives we're all growing in the garden of our souls and then watch the lessons blossom into fruitful living.

The Bible says of us believers that at the moment of salvation, the seed of God's own holy nature was placed within us, creating the potential for Him to do what only He can do: to produce something pure and sacred through us. He deposited a seed, "not of perishable seed but of imperishable" by His "living and enduring word" (1 Pet. 1:23).

But this seed—the new nature—needs to be nurtured, tended, and cultivated if we expect it to develop as it should. If the seed doesn't grow, you can't blame the seed. The problem is with the one who's been given the seed to care for and steward.

Here's another way to picture it. When Jerry and I caught our first ultrasound glimpse of each of the three little humans I once carried inside my belly all those years ago, we saw nothing more than something resembling a tiny dot the size of a cashew with a steadily flashing heartbeat. Today, these three sons of ours are growing into big, strong men. At twenty-one, nineteen, and fifteen years old, the days of holding them in my arms are long gone. Whenever I see them, I admit I still feel a ping of shock initially. I can't believe all that facial hair, muscle definition, and deep vocal resonance could possibly have emerged from what I first saw of them back then in my ob-gyn's office. Yet on that screen, in seed form, those little peanuts were already the big, tall, strapping, six-foot-three-inch men they've now become. They just needed to be given the chance to grow.

Goodness, Jerry and I have been far from perfect in our parenting, but we tried to take our job seriously in fostering an environment in our home that contributed toward helping them reach their full adult potential. They needed to be fed. (Lord, have mercy, did they ever!) They needed to be encouraged, corrected, guided, educated, and given grace as they took the time they needed to mature. With all these things in place—and more than all, the mercy of their heavenly Father in tow—these once babbling babies grew up into their physical, emotional, and mental uniqueness. They became (and are still becoming) what God had already encoded within their physical DNA. All we did as parents was to cooperate with the growth process.

It's a *cooperation*, see—that's the right word for it: *cooperating*. We cooperate with the Holy Spirit by creating the right environment in our heart for the seed of our spiritual identity to flourish. We clear the way for Him to grow us up in the direction He intends to take us. When we respond to His work in us, He grows us into followers He can lead to purposeful and fruitful living.

Now if I were you, I'd get ready to underline this next sentence. Here's how we cooperate with God in this indoor gardening project: we (1) renew our minds in His Word; (2) diligently cultivate a friendship with Jesus in prayer; (3) heed the conviction of the Spirit; (4) believe and obey Him so we don't grieve the Spirit or hinder His work.

These kinds of cooperative activities create a conducive space for spiritual growth to organically occur inside us. They're part of what the apostle Peter meant when he told us to "make every effort" to grow in Christ (2 Pet. 1:5). We prepare the soil of our hearts for the Holy Spirit to operate inside. We lay the groundwork for Him to turn our surrender into something that is both glorifying to Him and is life-giving, nourishing, and edifying to everyone around us. We don't *do* things to earn God's favor; we simply use what we know about our redeemed identity to participate with Him in His purpose of turning ordinary believers into bought-in, fruit-bearing disciples.

Salvation, you understand, is a gift. It is freely given to us by God's grace, to be received by faith in Christ as our Savior. Expensive for *Him* but a priceless gift to us.

Discipleship, however, is not a gift. Discipleship is a divine invitation, an opportunity for us to take this new identity we've been given in Christ and start making our attitudes and actions match up with it, so that our daily lives become congruent with it.

Our task is not to manufacture fruit, which is just our attempt at impressing other people or at seeking God's acceptance. Remember, *He* is the vine, responsible for the fruit the branch yields. Our charge is simply to agree with Him about what this seed of new life He's given us is capable of doing, to accept what He's recreated inside us, to abide in Him, and to offer Him full, unadulterated access to us. It is *His* work occurring in *our* readied soil.

This is the essence of discipleship.

And this is why a misunderstanding of our identity is such an inhibitor to His Holy Spirit. It makes us like the thorny ground in Jesus's parable of the seed, where "the worries of this age and the deceitfulness of wealth choke the word, and it becomes unfruitful" (Matt. 13:22). When the environment is unhealthy, the seed doesn't grow; the disciple bears no fruit. And then, knowing something is wrong, we start forcing ourselves to look and feel the way we think a person who's growing in Christ is supposed to look and feel—by doing more, by working harder. We strain and strive, trying to prove our faith is real. But the growth is fake and false. It fails us. Our life becomes ineffective. Then the enemy latches onto our frustration, accusing us of failing at a task we weren't even called to perform anyway.

We don't need to *do* things for God; we just need a heart and mind consistent with our identity. Dead to sin, alive to God. Accepted and forgiven. Free and filled. He can work with that. He can grow something in that garden.

The reason a disciple's life is marked by such a healthy, robust, and noticeable harvest—healthy from the ground up, in every area of her life—is because she's stopped being her own growth agent. She's learned to simply be His cooperator. The fruit you see is the fruit of the Holy Spirit.

The fruit of true discipleship, rooted in her new spiritual identity.

Surrendering All

All praise to God, the Father of our Lord Jesus Christ,
who has blessed us with every spiritual blessing in the
heavenly realms because we are united with Christ.
Ephesians 1:3 NLT

In what ways have you tended to underestimate your
spiritual identity? Who or what has contributed to this
distorted perspective, and what have been the repercus-
sions in your life?

_____

_____

_____

_____

_____

_____

_____

_____

_____

_____

Is the seed of new life that the Father deposited in you being malnourished or is it being strengthened? What are the contributing factors to your answer?

_____

_____

_____

_____

_____

_____

_____

_____

_____

_____

_____

_____

_____

_____

_____

What adjustments are you aware of and committed to make in order to ensure that you feed, nurture, and cultivate spiritual health moving forward?

_____

_____

_____

_____

_____

_____

_____

_____

_____

_____

_____

_____

_____

_____

For Further Reading
Luke 8:14–15 • Colossians 1:9–10 • Colossians 2:6–7

CHAPTER 4

Everything You're Becoming

Therefore, brothers and sisters, make every effort to confirm your calling and election, because if you do these things you will never stumble.

2 Peter 1:10

My son Jude is in high school now—a headstrong, fun-loving young man with an inquisitive mind and a noticeable interest in exploring possibilities and pushing boundaries. When I think back on his younger, elementary years, I see traces of these qualities stretching all the way to his earliest days in life.

I remember one occasion when he was only five or six. Our family was out shopping at a local mall. Needing to go to the second floor, we came to a set of escalators, and all of us stepped one by one onto the revolving stairs, beginning our slow but steady ascent. We were already well on our way when I looked around and realized Jude wasn't with us. Where did he go?

It didn't take long to find out. Directly across from us, where the adjoining escalator was located, Jude was taking a much more exhilarating ride to our second-floor destination. While the rest of us were basically standing still, letting the easy momentum of the escalator carry us upward, Jude had decided it would be far more interesting, and a lot more fun, to ride the rapids of the *down* escalator on his climb to the top. He'd apparently run around to the other side while we were getting aboard, and now he was breathlessly marching against the grain of the downward-moving staircase, as well as against the traffic of annoyed mall shoppers who were no doubt wondering what kind of terrible mother would let her child do this.

Startled, I immediately called out to him and told him to let the escalator bring him back down—the way everybody else was doing it, the way everybody else was facing—then to come around here and get on the *up* escalator instead. He smiled his sheepish grin, shrugged his little shoulders, turned himself around, and let the machine do what the machine does. It brought him down to the ground without a fight.

Because going *down* was the direction it was headed.

I chuckle thinking back to that day, recalling my precocious son's adventure. I can still see him charging and chopping against the undertow of that escalator. He was being so intentional, so deliberate, so consistent, putting one brave foot in front of the other. He was investing so much hard work and extra effort into achieving his goal:

going *up* a bank of stairs that were continually going *down*, taking him *opposite* the direction he wanted to go.

Neutrality wasn't an option for him in the position where he'd put himself. To stop moving and *not* climb upward was to automatically be taken down by it. Because when you're standing on something that's moving downward, you don't need to be doing anything wrong to lose ground. You don't need to be doing anything at all. It requires no effort just to roll with it.

But going up does.

∽

We are standing on a planet, in a culture, that is going downward. And all of humanity is going with it. You can see it happening all around us, the natural descent into decadence and decay. From environmental issues to economic trends to the raw enmity between people groups and warring nations, everything seems to be hurtling downhill without the brakes on.

You see it most of all in the trajectory of human morality, spiraling down at an alarming, unprecedented rate of speed. The decay of cultural decency is blatant, as well as the decline of respect for the values and ideals championed by the Scriptures and reverenced by those of us who follow Jesus. Society's ethical compass is clearly pointed south because "the whole world is under the sway of the evil one" (1 John 5:19). People are not only *tolerant* of evil but are *in love* with it—"lovers of self," "lovers of pleasure"—just as the Bible told us to expect from these days (2 Tim. 3:1–5). We shouldn't be surprised by this reality—seeing the world applaud the salacious, support the scandalous, and consistently perpetuate ideas and ideals that are indecent—but we do need to stay aware of it so we can be vigilant about our response to it.

Because like Jude on the down-going escalator, neutrality is not an option.

We cannot stand here assuming we can ride along with the current and just naturally elevate toward Christlikeness. Our desire for spiritual maturity, our focus on kingdom-minded priorities, runs completely opposite to the direction the world is trending.

So we disciples who march to a different drumbeat, who serve a different King, and who pursue a different purpose should brace for an upstream swim. Not that the effort to do so is ours to originate and empower. It is always Christ's doing. But the direction He is taking us as branches on the vine is a stab against the prevailing winds that are pushing back on us as believers, especially on us as disciples. And we must be willing to go there, to grow there, to "walk worthy of the calling [we] have received" (Eph. 4:1). To *step up*. To make choices, choose behaviors, and exhibit the restraint required to align ourselves with the work His Spirit is doing in and through us. We are responsible for stepping up into this endeavor. The ride down is easy, but the walk up is tenacious. It requires consistency. It takes intentionality.

It involves "effort."

I mentioned this word to you in the previous chapter, just as it appears in the writings of Peter the apostle. The reason I've waited till now to break it out for you is because I didn't want you to hear "effort" and feel the mounting pressure: "Oh, no, something else for me to do." Because, I know, you're doing a million things already. All you need is another seven balls to juggle, right? That's not what this chapter's list of biblical stairsteps is supposed to feel like for us as disciples—another mountain to move, another mountain to climb. So before I reach the part where Peter tells us to "make every effort" in running uphill against the confrontational force of our world and our flesh and our enemy, let's do what we should always do when reading the Word: ask the Spirit to help us see it in context.

The biblical urging to "make every effort" comes along for us in 2 Peter 1:5, but the preamble to this appeal comes in verses 3–4, where he talks about the very things you and I have already addressed on every page so far of this book.

- God's "divine power" that has already "given us everything required for life and godliness"

- How He's "called us by his own glory and goodness" to be His beloved, adopted children
- The "very great and precious promises" that are ours by being in relationship with Him . . .
- . . . which allow us to "share in the divine nature," to freely cooperate with Him . . .
- . . . in "escaping the corruption that is in the world because of evil desire"

"Make every effort" is not the beginning point. "Get busy" is not the opening line of Peter's speech. The "very reason" we can "make every effort" are the facts of verses 3–4, the solid ground of what we've been given and the ongoing empowerment we receive from Him every day. "For it is [not your strength, but it is] God who is effectively at work in you, both to will and to work [that is, strengthening, energizing, and creating in you the longing and the ability to fulfill your purpose] for His good pleasure" (Phil. 2:13 AMP). That's our motivation and permission not to just stand here, stuck in idle, squandering all this holy energy and investment.

Let's dare to be a Jude, I say—defying gravity, staying curious about the potential we've been given, finding out what's possible if we decide we've already seen this movie, the one where we float along in the tide long enough until we wash up on a distant shoreline of indifference or apathy or skepticism or sin, somewhere we never intended to go.

Instead, let's see what this sacred vine can do when we truly abide in it. Let's see what this new identity of ours can do when we cooperate with it and surrender to our Lord. Let's see if we really do gain our lives when we divorce ourselves from those treasured things (and those treasured sins) that we don't think we can live without, and we marry ourselves to the promise Jesus makes to every disciple who is finally willing to surrender all.

"For this very reason," Peter said, let's "make every effort" to be a disciple who is branching out into all these different areas, growing a whole bunch of different kinds of desirable fruit, supplementing our . . .

> faith with virtue, and virtue with knowledge, and knowledge with self-control, and self-control with steadfastness, and steadfastness with godliness, and godliness with brotherly affection, and brotherly affection with love. (2 Pet. 1:5–7 ESV)

Virtue

Let's begin our journey here: "Make every effort to supplement your faith with virtue" (v. 5 ESV). Some translations call it "goodness" or, more formally, "moral excellence" (NASB). Either way, the original Greek word refers to something or someone that is fulfilling its purpose for existence. When something has *virtue*, it is functioning the way its manufacturer intended. It is operating according to its design. It is accomplishing what it was created to do.

So, when a car drives, it is exhibiting virtue. When a fish swims, it is exhibiting virtue. When a bird flies, a bell chimes, a band plays, or a bicycle rides, it is expressing its internal virtue.

What, then, does a follower of Christ do to show she has virtue, to invoke this sort of obvious recognition from people who see her? What is she created to accomplish? What does a living disciple do, everywhere she goes?

> Whether you eat or drink, or *whatever you do*, do everything for the glory of God.
> (1 Cor. 10:31, emphasis added)

Glorifying God is the overarching purpose, the highest goal for a follower of Jesus. In all the fundamental behaviors of life—right down to our eating and our drinking—we were created to be living, breathing, walking billboards for our Creator. This, in essence, is what glorifying God means. It means to advertise Him, to reflect His ideals, and to draw attention to Him.

Sadly, many people have relegated the overt glorifying of the Lord to those who serve in full-time ministry. But elevating God to a position of central focus isn't just for vocational ministers, preachers, and evangelists. Oh, they need to do it, too. But this same calling goes for every person who calls herself a disciple. She's been created to operate with God-honoring excellence in whatever sector of life she's been assigned.

- The doctor should bring attention to her reliance on God even while she tends to her patients.
- The lawyer should see each client as a divine assignment while she represents them in the courtroom.
- The teacher should appropriately and creatively utilize her influence to point her students to Christ and to His principles.
- The entrepreneur should build her businesses with a sturdy underpinning of integrity that reflects the character of her Father, even while she generates income.
- The mother should understand that the joyful, exhausting responsibility of raising those small children is her holy opportunity to instill in them God's principles for living. She is God's partner in shaping their lives to honor Him.

- The actor, poet, or songwriter should see every script, monologue, or lyric as her chance to reflect Christ's ideals and to impact her industry by the excellence of her hardworking creativity.
- The social justice activist should advocate for the marginalized and the underserved while facilitating societal change that steers culture back toward biblical principles. And she should do it all unashamedly in the name of Jesus, for the glory of God alone.

The disciple understands there is no separation between the sacred part of her life and the secular part—the Sunday part and the Monday-through-Saturday part. For her, all of it is sacred. The compass reading on everything she is and everything she does, on everything she's been assigned to do, is continually pointed in the direction of His glory.

Consider the following powerful revelation.

In the Hebrew language, the term used to convey "work" and "worship" is not two different words, like it is in our English language. Instead, both are summed up in the word *avodah*. Throughout the Scriptures, this noun is used more than 1,000 times to express the distinct yet intertwined connection between these aspects of life. This unity of thought can enlarge our understanding of worship from merely singing songs in church, and it can also elevate our perception of what God intended our work to produce. For ancient Hebrews, there was a seamless nature between their daily toil and their service to and worship of Yahweh. These acts were not divided up into separate categories of life. Instead, they were considered to be one and the same. Their work, when accomplished with integrity and unto God, was their worship and their service to Him.

There's *virtue* in maintaining this kind of perspective.

But, boy, is it countercultural in our Western culture that has segmented these aspects of living. Being focused on His glory instead of your own is not the direction all the other people on the escalator are going. But when you see this priority in someone—especially someone who is excelling at their craft or in their field—the difference is noticeable and unforgettable.

I'll never forget being in a hospital room with a family member who was being prepped for a fairly serious surgical procedure. Nurses had been coming in and out for several nervous hours, monitoring vital signs, filling out paperwork, inserting IV lines, administering medications. But just when we thought the next face coming through the door would be the person responsible for wheeling the patient to the operating room, the surgeon stepped into the room himself.

His smile was peaceful. His countenance was calm. He asked both of us if we had any questions, and he patiently answered them all.

He then asked us a question. "Would it be alright if I prayed for you before we begin?" Yes, of course! And with that, he bowed his head, laid his skilled hand on my loved one's shoulder, and asked the Lord to preside over every aspect of the procedure and to be glorified through the outcome.

He may have been a doctor with a scalpel, but his scrubs were disguising a devoted disciple. And yet we could clearly recognize him because his virtue was showing. He was a spectacular example of what Jesus told all His followers to do: "Let your light shine before others, so that they may see your good works and give glory to your Father in heaven" (Matt. 5:16).

Every disciple, by *virtue* of our calling, is here to do the same thing as every other disciple: to honor God, to advance His kingdom, to look for ways to broadcast His glory through the sphere He's entrusted us to work and live inside. When we do this—instead of feverishly pursuing the markers of success applauded by our culture as our ultimate priority—we're expressing virtue. We're stepping up into the real purpose for which we were created. And for the disciple, there's no greater source of fulfillment than that.

Knowledge

When Jerry and I started dating, one of the ways I knew how seriously he felt about me was not just in how he would go out of his way to spend time with me but also because of what he wanted to talk about when we were together.

Whether during our long hours on the phone or over the meals we shared when we went out, he was always asking me questions to find out about my life, about who I was. He wanted to know more about me—just as I wanted to know more about him—about this other person we were each falling in love with.

When Peter tells us to pursue "knowledge" (2 Pet. 1:5), he's not talking about simply getting smarter. Instead, he's referring to building an intimate knowledge about the person of Jesus: who He is, what His character entails, what His heart reflects. Being smart is applaudable, but a person can know facts about the Scriptures and the history surrounding it without having a deeply rooted friendship with Jesus. To be disciples who keep our footing and make forward progress in a culture gone cliff-diving, it's not enough to generally know information. We need to know *Jesus*—not a program, not denominational politics, not the various rules and regulations expected of our religious affiliation. The aim of the disciple, as both

Peter and Paul tell us, is to become as deeply acquainted with Jesus as humanly possible throughout our lifetime.

My goal is to know him. (Phil 3:10)

This declaration of the apostle Paul is the daily ambition of a true disciple: to know everything about this Person we are surrendering our lives to.

We are in a love relationship with Jesus. And His love letter to us—the Bible—is an expression of His commitment to us and His pursuit of us. So whenever we're reading, the end goal is not to know the Bible itself; the goal is to know the Author of it. Like any love letter, it's been written to point us back to the Lover who wrote the words, not just to fill our head with facts.

Without a doubt, He has given us ways to know Him, most importantly through the Scriptures (John 5:39) and through the inner witness of His Spirit, who "takes from what is mine" and declares God's truth to us (John 16:15), whose assignment is to "teach you all things and remind you of everything I have told you" (John 14:26). He's given us prayer as well, the every-moment opportunity to talk with Him, knowing He's invited us not only into His hearing but also to pause and hear His heart spoken back to us.

It's an "effort," yes, but the love makes it worth it. The same love that compelled Jerry to drive miles out of his way to see me should drive us to turn off our devices and curl up with the Good Book. The same attitude that made him see inconveniences as investments in our growing relationship should compel us to invest time with our Savior, time we'd ordinarily waste worrying about ourselves.

When I would tell Jerry that he didn't need to go to such lengths to come see me, he would say it was his pleasure, that he was glad to do it. The big things, the small things—they were all worth the effort of getting to know me. Wow. I didn't deserve it. But Jesus does. And He wants us to know Him, to become more deeply acquainted with Him. He wants us to grow the kind of relationship that develops not from putting more church duties on our calendar but from just spending time with Him, to "grow in the grace and knowledge of our Lord and Savior Jesus Christ. To him be the glory both now and to the day of eternity" (2 Pet. 3:18).

Making every effort to add *knowledge* to our *virtue*.

Self-control

It doesn't take a close watcher of current events to tell us our world has decided the key to happiness and contentment is found in satiating every desire, in expecting instant gratification, in relentlessly pursuing our own interests at any cost. It does, however, take a devoted disciple of Jesus to hear and respond with the tempered and sober lifestyle He has called us to pursue.

Discipleship demands restraint.

A control of self.

Every one of us lives with tendencies, desires, and proclivities that our flesh just naturally leans toward. And, by themselves, many of these desires are not sinful. The desires to earn or to eat, to have fun or to have sex, are not inherently sinful motivations for us to quash and eliminate. Even the desire for feeling strong emotions and expressing them is not sinful on its own.

Desires don't make us sinners; desires make us human. Peter is not suggesting you should no longer have desires; he is saying that as Christ's disciple, your desires should no longer have you.

Paul said it like this:

> "Everything is permissible for me," but not everything is beneficial. "Everything is permissible for me," but I will not be mastered by anything. (1 Cor. 6:12)

This was his way of saying that the only controlling power in our lives should be the power of the Holy Spirit. "For the flesh desires what is against the Spirit, and the Spirit desires what is against the flesh; these are opposed to each other, so that you don't do what you want" (Gal. 5:17).

Our desires, in other words, can make fine servants, but they always make horrible masters. By yielding them *all* to God, He enables us to restrain these desires from devolving into sins—overworking, overeating, overreacting, engaging in sexual immorality—and He redeploys them in ways that bring glory to God. He brings them all under the umbrella of our chief desire: our desire for knowing and loving and walking with Jesus.

"The fruit of the Spirit is . . ." many things, and you should expect to experience all of them. They grow simultaneously on the branch of your abiding trust in Christ. One of them is the fruit of "self-control" (Gal. 5:23). And though this fruit often seems the hardest to obtain—and is impossible to grow on our own—God causes its fruit to grow in us the same way as all the others.

The more we lean back on Him, that's how much more He propels us forward. And pretty soon, in areas where we've failed a thousand times ourselves, He's supernaturally enabling the climb up the down escalator. He's empowering us to make broader leaps and strides toward reining in our temper, toward governing our impulses, toward bridling our tongues—actually *doing* things (or *not* doing things) that we'd never been able to consistently do or not do before. All because we've stopped giving our desires final decision-making power. We've turned them over to new management. And the difference is night and day.

It's not lost on me that this passage from 2 Peter was written by Simon Peter, who was hardly the poster child for self-control. On the Mount of Transfiguration, while

Jesus was glistening in glory, Peter was blabbing about
building a retreat center for Moses and Elijah. When Jesus
was preparing the disciples for His approaching death,
Peter went on record as saying he would never allow such
a thing. "'Even if everyone else falls away because of you,
I will never fall away. . . . Even if I have to die with you,'
Peter told him. 'I will never deny you'" (Matt. 26:33, 35).
And, of course, you remember how that went.

And yet, something happened to him to change him.
The Peter of this passage doesn't sound like the same
man who, when Jesus told him how he would one day
suffer death for being His disciple, pointed to John and
said, "Lord, what about him?" (John 21:21). He'd made
a determined effort over his years of following Christ to
forsake one of his most besetting sins, by surrendering it
to the life-changing power of Jesus. Night-and-day difference indeed. God can overhaul character traits in us
we never thought possible. When we are committed to
cooperate.

Think of the effort each of us has been willing to
implement in areas of our lives that we may have allowed
to get out of control in one season or another. When we
feel our weight is too heavy and we want to lose some of
it to get healthier, we may keep a meticulous food journal,
writing down everything we've eaten through the day to
make sure we stay under a predetermined calorie count.
We'll even stop buying certain foods altogether at the

grocery so they're not in the pantry or fridge to tempt us. I know one woman who decided to change her driving route to work each day so it wouldn't take her past the local Krispy Kreme shop whenever the "Hot Doughnuts" sign was illuminated!

This is all good. Good cooperation. Things like enlisting an accountability source. Paying for a gym membership, perhaps even hiring a personal trainer. Cutting up a credit card or working with a financial advisor to stick with a budget. It proves we're willing to "make every effort" when we want something bad enough. We've been known to establish all kinds of intentional strategies to assist us in being self-controlled in many different areas of our lives.

Peter's just saying, let's be equally intentional—more intentional—about desiring the health of our souls and our spirits, in the same ways we often commit to the health of our bodies and our finances. Without a Spirit-generated restraint at work in us, we will constantly over-indulge in the good things we're blessed to enjoy, as well as routinely embrace the evil things that can only bring us harm.

In fact, this determined discipline, practiced consistently throughout the ebbs and flows of each season and circumstance of our lives, will help us add a fourth attribute to our catalog of spiritual growth.

Steadfastness

As I round out my forties and head toward my fiftieth birthday, I find myself increasingly aware of, endeared to, and moved by disciples who've exhibited perseverance and who are marked by the character trait of "endurance" (2 Pet. 1:6). People who are steadfast.

Like you, I've walked through my own hills and valleys, my own peaks and plateaus, and have had a lot of opportunities to watch others go through ups and downs as well. How rare are the examples of people who walk through their problems with perseverance, who endure them faithfully enough to testify to God's goodness and give Him glory for it on the other side. Or, even more astounding, they testify and give Him glory before the other side materializes. Even if the other side never appears at all.

What an encouraging example they are—people who may not be famous, rich, or widely recognizable, but they have been "steadfast, immovable, always excelling in the Lord's work" (1 Cor. 15:58).

They've *persevered*. I'm drawn to it, captivated by it, and inspired because of it.

Instead of throwing in the towel, instead of succumbing to skepticism and bitterness, these people have endured by the power of the Holy Spirit. They've stayed the course. They've kept their hand to the plow. They've

remained steady and consistent with their profession of
faith. They've forged ahead against resistance.

That's what makes their examples so encouraging—
because *perseverance* implies the reality of resistance.
There's opposition they've pressed through. There's a
pile of personal, descending escalator steps that have
made their trek even harder than it already was. Being
steadfast is a struggle. It requires muscle, lung capacity,
and willpower.

In nearly every line of Peter's letters—both 1 Peter
and 2 Peter—you'll read about the many points of resistance every surrendered follower of Christ is absolutely
assured of facing. But whatever those sticking points and
persecutions may look like in your life, the Spirit is there
to keep you going forward. "Make every effort," I think
Peter would tell you, to make the Lord's efforts in you the
hardbought, fruit-bearing kind that are becoming of His
disciples.

- In a valley year in your marriage. *Persevere.*
- In the umpteenth year of still being single.
  Persevere.
- In a lean year of building your business.
  Persevere.
- In your toughest year yet in parenting.
  Persevere.

- In the third major house repair this year. *Persevere.*
- In a trying year of church planting and restructuring. *Persevere.*

Don't quit now. By the Spirit's power within you, keep stepping up. Day by day. Moment by moment. He is refining you in this. He is strengthening you through this. And He is being glorified by your commitment to endure.

It's a *choice* we must make, yes—to "make every effort," to be resolved, to maintain the tenacity and steadfastness of our faith. We make up our mind. We will not become hard-hearted, vengeful, cold, or resentful. We will not give up, cave in, let go, or walk away. We will endure with the sustaining strength of God's Spirit. We will persevere until He calls us home.

But to help us achieve such a difficult ambition, we'll need something all the people of resolution and perseverance whom I admire possess, a quality each of them holds in common with the rest. It's the single thread that weaves all these people's unique stories and dynamics together.

Godliness

The term itself carries a sacred weight: "godliness" (2 Pet. 1:7). We all want to see more of it looking back at us in the mirror each day. But if it sounds a little too theoretical, hard to bring down into practical use, think of godliness as being a *God-centered lifestyle*, one that constantly and consistently orbits around an awareness that He is near, that He is present.

I told you about our young Jude at the beginning of this chapter, but I don't mind reporting he is no longer the little kid I needed to talk down off the escalator. He is now a fifteen-year-old teenager. And as of his latest birthday, he's now the newest (and thankfully the last) young driver in our family.

Freeway driving is his favorite. He feels a bit more unrestricted on the wide-open lanes of the highway. I'm glad to say he's a fairly cautious driver, but he does tend to accelerate more than his mama would prefer.

Whenever I'm riding with him and I ask him to please slow down, he usually snickers and teases me. He says I'm one of those "older ladies" now who thinks any speed exceeding thirty miles per hour is too fast.

But I've found his interaction with the gas pedal is different when he is sailing along on the freeway and notices a police officer's car ahead in the line of traffic or parked in the median. As soon as he spots one of those familiar black-and-white cruisers pulled over on the shoulder, armed with radar-gun capabilities, I can see the visible signs of awareness begin to spark. First, he straightens those shoulders, while simultaneously easing up on that heavy foot. He checks his speedometer to make sure he's within the posted limits, and his engaged brain—which may have been on autopilot—kicks into full gear, suddenly becoming intently aware of all his surroundings.

You know how this feels, not just for young fifteen-year-old drivers but for grown folks like us too. Becoming aware of the patrolman's presence makes us more aware of ourselves and of our driving. The trooper in question doesn't even need to pull us over or make any move toward threatening us with a ticket. Just *being there* is all it takes to have an immediate effect on the way we operate our vehicle.

Or so I've heard.

A godly person is someone who is aware of the presence of God as she goes throughout her day. She is, to use a couple more words that Peter repeats and wants to impress upon us, "alert" and "sober-minded" (1 Pet. 4:7; 5:8). The godly woman knows, even when no one is watching, even when she is physically alone with her thoughts and her actions, *God* is there.

"Even the darkness is not dark to you," she remembers about Him. "The night shines like the day; darkness and light are alike to you" (Ps. 139:12). The God who comforts her because He is never far away is the same God whose ever-closeness wakes her up to behaviors, attitudes, and responses she'd never choose if she thought there was any chance of being seen and known.

That's *godliness*. And that's a helpful, cooperative effort we can make toward becoming a surrendered disciple. Knowing that God is with us reminds us of our desire to honor Him in all our thoughts and actions, a desire that slips down our priority list whenever we allow other desires to assume the driver's seat.

Do you see how all these supplemental essentials blend together to complete our wholehearted bent toward following Him? We need them all: *virtue, knowledge, self-control, perseverance*. Also *godliness*. His presence awakens us out of our spiritual doldrums and invites us to live well for His glory and to live with the added beauty of brotherly affection.

Brotherly Affection

These two words—"brotherly affection" (2 Pet. 1:7) or brotherly kindness—come from two original Greek words: *phileo* and *adolphus*. We derive the city name "Philadelphia" from them which, as you know, is represented in Philly's nickname: "The City of Brotherly Love."

In other words, this is a family term. It refers to brothers and sisters linked together by a familial bond.

When you were born again, you were born into a family that includes other children. You are not an only child, and neither am I. We have spiritual siblings in Christ, and our posture toward these extended family members should be love.

And *kindness.*

Godliness feeds naturally into this calling of brotherly kindness. A mean-spirited saint is, more than anything, someone who's lost sight of being surrounded and indwelt by God's divine nature. The unawareness comes out in ugliness. Lack of godliness is one of the central places where a lack of kindness stems from.

And if we ever needed to be admonished, challenged, and corrected about anything as a Christian family today—if there's an area where the importance of our stepping up is currently most acute—I believe it's in this matter of brotherly kindness. It's imperative we allow the Spirit to transform our treatment of one another not only in private but in our public digital spaces and social media platforms. The state of our cultural discourse has reached deplorable lows.

Too many are spewing vitriol, hatred, contempt, and cruelty into these virtual gathering places, doing it with a level of ease and comfortability that is astounding to behold and, when done in the name of defending Christ, an affront to our heavenly Father. He who's gone to such enormous lengths to bridge the gap between ourselves and a holy God has not made secret the fact that He did it also to bridge the gap between ourselves and others. The attitude He prizes in our relationships with one another is "unity" (Col. 3:14), a desire Paul accentuated with a "make every effort" of his own (Eph. 4:3 NLT). The bullying, unkindness, and discord we all see—the lack of grace and patience we too often hear expressed—in no way reflects the grace and patience we've been afforded through Christ.

I'll just say it bluntly and unapologetically: the division among us in the body of Christ is demonic. Anyone with spiritual eyes to see is visibly aware of the enemy's influence on us, the way he seeks to sow division and disunity. He does it one race against another, one political persuasion against another, one church denomination against another—anything to ignite within us an angry contempt toward our own brothers and sisters in Christ.

And it's time we stopped giving him the kindling for that fire. It's time we "make every effort" to end his initiative of nastiness.

I've often told my three sons, whenever they've gotten into fights or arguments with one another, "You don't have to agree with each other in order to be kind to each other." The same is true for us in the family of Christ. Unity does not mean uniformity; it simply means oneness of purpose. And for us—for all of us—our purpose and goal should be the same. We exist to glorify God. We must keep His glory in the forefront, even when we're not in full agreement on certain details in secondary issues of doctrine or opinion.

In Jesus's name and for the sake of His glory, *be kind*.

To be clear, this phrase—"brotherly kindness"—doesn't carry the same meaning as "niceness." Being nice is just a state of being. You can be *nice*; you can be *not* nice. Niceness is not necessarily a virtue. The Scripture doesn't make a big deal out of telling us to be nice. But the Lord does directly exhort us to be "kind," which is an expression of what we *do*.

Being nice? Pssh. Lots of people are nice simply by temperament.

But being kind? Kindness is love in action. By intention. It requires effort.

Peter is telling us, as disciples, to overtly, proactively express and extend kind overtures to others.

None of us really has any idea, when our paths cross with other people, what the first part of their day was like before we stood across from them. Or the first part of their *life*, for that matter. We don't know the devils they've faced, the hardships they've overcome, or the deserts they've traveled through before arriving here on the landscape of our lives. Yet the Spirit of God has providentially brought us together with them. The active kindness we offer them at this precise hour could be the difference between someone calling it quits or choosing to live another day.

So *make every effort*. That's what disciples do. They deliberately shine a simple smile. They offer a simple gift, even if it's just the gift of eye contact and personal attention. They engage other people in edifying conversation, and they offer to listen, not like others who only seem interested in shutting them down.

Be brotherly. Be sisterly. Be kind and generous of spirit.

Live a kind life on purpose. In love. And start today.

Love

Isn't this always where everything we do should be headed? Not just *phileo* love—brotherly kindness love—but agape love. God's love. This love reflects the Father's love for us, how He "proves his own love [*agape*] for us in that while we were still sinners, Christ died for us" (Rom. 5:8). Sacrificial love. Unwarranted love. Unexpected love. Unbelievable love. At least it would be unbelievable if anyone else besides God was doing it.

Or anyone His Spirit was empowering to love like He loves.

That's you and me, making every effort to make the unselfish decision to compassionately, fearlessly, and righteously meet the needs of another without expecting anything in return. As Jesus said,

> "By this everyone will know that you are
> my disciples, if you love one another." (John
> 13:35)

Yes, people know *agape* love when they see it.

> Love is patient, love is kind. Love does not
> envy, is not boastful, is not arrogant, is not
> rude, is not self-seeking, is not irritable, and
> does not keep a record of wrongs. Love finds
> no joy in unrighteousness but rejoices in the
> truth. It bears all things, believes all things,
> hopes all things, endures all things.
> Love never ends. (1 Cor. 13:4–8)

- It has *virtue*, a purposeful intent to glorify God.
- It indicates a living and vibrant *knowledge* of Christ.
- It is characterized by being unselfishly *self-controlled*.
- It works tenaciously, yet tenderly, to *persevere*.
- It identifies a person committed to *godliness*.
- It marries beautifully with *brotherly kindness*.

These things are everything a disciple wants God to make of her life.

And she's prepared to "make every effort" to join Him in the process.

Peter, speaking truth inspired by the Holy Spirit, says there's a promise in store for us disciples who are diligent to *make every effort.* . . .

> For if you possess these qualities in increasing measure, they will keep you from being useless or unfruitful in the knowledge of our Lord Jesus Christ. (2 Pet. 1:8)

In other words, stepping up into these qualities makes us fruitful, useful for kingdom purpose, and it supports the full potential of our own spiritual growth. Conversely, when we do not make the effort to increase these qualities, we hurt ourselves, our spiritual growth is stunted, and we flounder below the level of abundant life we were redeemed to experience.

We don't just steal blessing from *others* when we treat them unkindly, and we don't just steal glory from *God* when we quench the life of His Spirit. We don't just pass up the opportunity for our lives to inspire worship for the One who does such amazing things through such average people like us. We steal from *ourselves*. We short-circuit our own spiritual capacity for maturing and abounding in Christ.

But when you consistently *add* all these treasures of character to your faith, God does something extremely remarkable with the math. The Bible says He will "*multiply* your seed and increase the harvest of your righteousness" (2 Cor. 9:10, emphasis added). He multiplies all of it exponentially back to you faster than you can pour out the offering of your surrendered service to Him.

It doesn't mean the down escalator won't always be a challenge, but it does mean God has created a path for you where you can scale the descending steps and outpace their downward pull.

By His Spirit.

And for His glory.

Surrendering All

May God give you more and more grace
and peace as you grow in your knowledge
of God and Jesus our Lord.
2 Peter 1:2 NLT

In what ways do you most notice the decline in culture?
How do these issues impact you personally?

_____

_____

_____

_____

_____

_____

_____

_____

_____

_____

_____

_____

Of the seven qualities Peter mentions, prayerfully consider: Which three do you most need to "step up"? How
is the Holy Spirit leading you to begin making progress
on them in the next twenty-four hours?

_____

_____

_____

_____

_____

_____

_____

_____

_____

_____

_____

_____

_____

_____

How is the Lord asking you to find a balance between (1) resting in Him, trusting His work in you, and (2) putting forth the effort to facilitate your own spiritual growth?

_____

_____

_____

_____

_____

_____

_____

_____

_____

_____

_____

_____

_____

_____

For Further Reading
1 Corinthians 15:58 • Philippians 2:12–16 • 2 Peter 3:18

Everything You Want

Take delight in the LORD, and he will
give you your heart's desires.
Psalm 37:4

At our home, we had a long-standing rule. When our sons woke up in the morning or came home from school or an activity, they were to ask their father or me, "Is there anything I can do to help?" before moving on with their day. It's a short sentence, but it comes with a long impact. And it stretches a lot farther than dinner dishes and laundry loads. It's a training in courtesy really, important in shaping them as young boys into the young men they are becoming.

Consider the question: Is there anything I can do to help? It requires them to think about the needs of others and to resist the tendency toward self-centeredness that exists in all of us. When they're at home, living in a space where they derive ongoing care and benefit, I don't want them just observing others busily working to prepare meals or clean rooms or organize spaces or keep a house running and not pause to ask if they can offer any support.

I want them accustomed to the perspective shift that
focuses on our family dynamic instead of being focused
solely on themselves. So for as long as I can remember,
we've demanded they take note of what's happening
around them and ask the question, "Can I help?"

And as you would expect, they love it!

(I wish we were together right now so you could hear
the sarcasm in my voice.)

I don't know many teenage boys (and some of ours
are at university now and only come home periodically)
who *want* to help their mom with an eager and enthusiastic countenance. I'm sure some exist, somewhere in
the world, somewhere in the wild, but not at our address.
My sons, throughout their growing-up years, most often
attempted to avoid the question altogether. Instead,
they'd offer a quick hello when they got home, then race
past me in the hope I'd forgotten the expectation. But
with one raise of my mama eyebrow, they'd know for sure
I recognized the omission. *Busted.* Only then would they
reluctantly ask me the question I wanted to hear but usually in a low grumble that was nearly indiscernible. They
said it with their shoulders slumped forward, their energy
level low, and (if they had the nerve) a bit of an eye roll.

Any of these reactions revealed to me the real state
of their heart. Even though they were doing what I'd
required, their attitudes disclosed to me that their heart

was not aligned with their actions. They viewed this as an obligation—"because Mom is making me"—not a delight.

Even then I still required it. I still require it today. But nothing satisfies my heart more than when I hear those words from them and can tell at a glance, from the look on their faces to the posture of their bodies, "Can I help?" is coming from a place of genuine gratitude and willingness.

I can do something with that. My future daughters-in-law can do something with that, with a husband who notices the effort his wife is investing in their home and relationship instead of showing up and expecting the world to revolve around him.

And God can do something with a person whose *delight* is in Him, giving Him opportunity to mold her heart's *desire* into that of a fully surrendered disciple.

❧

Holy affection cannot be manufactured. Any self-reliant attempt to initiate or rejuvenate a fervent love in our hearts for God and a surrender to His will can only result in manifesting one of two extremes: *emotionalism* or *legalism*.

Sometimes we just like how being a Christian feels. We can get caught up in worship and declare our love for Him because of all He's done for us. And that'll hold us for a while, until we no longer feel it anymore, at least not strongly enough to drown out the inner tug on our heart that delights in serving ourselves. Oh, we'll probably still paste on plastic Sunday smiles and lift mechanical holy hands with those around us, appearing to have the heart-felt love for God we know we're supposed to possess. But it's not a sustainable posture because it's not a disciple's passion.

Or we'll lean toward the pharisaical disposition of rule-keeping. We'll craft our own set of regulations or follow an exaggerated version of what the Scriptures require, being proud of what we're doing while being judgmental of what others are not. But even in somewhat succeeding at maintaining these external standards, our appearance of passion will not consistently mask how hard-hearted and skeptical and callous we've become underneath. We'll busy ourselves with unending tasks that eventually become an inadequate veneer, a shallow and easily shattered disguise for the lack of love for Jesus we genuinely feel. Despite all our best trying and effort, the true state of our souls will ultimately win out and cause our manufactured façade to crumble. We cannot consistently do something over the long haul that we're not passionate about.

It becomes duty without devotion.

And it's unbecoming of a disciple.

"I delight to do your will, my God," said David, speaking prophetically of Christ in the Old Testament (Ps. 40:8). "My food is to do the will of him who sent me and to finish his work," said Jesus Himself, speaking in the New Testament (John 4:34).

As His disciple today, the question becomes: *How can our obedience to Him spring up from a deeply rooted love and affection for Him?*

Leave it to one of His original twelve disciples to show us the way.

John the apostle, whose writings appear throughout the New Testament, was himself an ideal example of how disciples are made. During Jesus's earthly ministry, multitudes followed Him and witnessed Him from afar, in the crowds, by the thousands, from a distance. Then Scripture speaks about "seventy-two" of them He "appointed" into His service (Luke 10:1), people who enjoyed a more close-up opportunity to watch His ministry unfold as He traveled around. Within this larger group, of course, were "twelve" He specifically named as His "apostles" (Luke 6:13), whose relationship with Him was more personal still. Then out of these twelve, Jesus invited three into an even tighter sphere with Him. "Peter, James, and his brother John" were allowed to witness with Him such deeply intimate, holy events as the transfiguration, alongside Moses and Elijah (Matt. 17:1). More than anyone else in those broader groupings of followers, these three were included as eyewitnesses to special moments with Christ that marked them in unforgettable ways.

But out of all these circles of association, there seemed to be one person He poured into in a unique way. John referred to himself as "the one Jesus loved," the disciple who, more than the others, was "reclining close beside Jesus" at their Last Supper together on the eve of Christ's crucifixion (John 13:23).

To this "one," God gave the words and experiences that became the biblical book we now call the Revelation. Profound and prophetic, it is at once a clear picture of Jesus and also a clarion call to His followers about what being His faithful, hopeful, enduring disciples truly entails. The book opens with such an overpowering demonstration of Christ's glory and holy purity that John "fell at his feet like a dead man" (Rev. 1:17). But Jesus, in the Spirit, helped His friend to his feet and gave him a series of messages to share with seven different churches throughout the world of that day and, thankfully, of ours.

Starting with this message about the state of the heart. About passion. About *first* love.

> I know your deeds and your labor and per-
> severance, and that you cannot tolerate evil
> people, and you have put those who call
> themselves apostles to the test, and they are
> not, and you found them to be false; and

you have perseverance and have endured on account of My name, and have not become weary. But I have this against you, *that you have left your first love.* (Rev. 2:2–4 NASB, emphasis added)

This church, the church at Ephesus, was in a peculiar and delicate position. Ephesus was a thriving seaport on the western coast of the Aegean Sea, one of the most influential cities of its time. It boasted a convergence of economic stability, educational prowess, and political power. And it was proudly pagan—the epicenter of idol worship to the Greek goddess Artemis, known to the Romans as Diana. Their reverence of her was clearly displayed in the spectacular edifice built to honor her and to house her image. The temple of Artemis was so significant that it was considered one of the Seven Wonders of the Ancient World.

Into this mecca of influence, the fledgling Christian church was birthed by the apostle Paul and then cultivated by Priscilla and Aquila. Its growth was so remarkable that the effect of it began to upset the local economy. New converts stopped buying the carefully crafted idols that were sold in the market center, which the local artisans depended on for their livelihood. In other words, the church at Ephesus was making a major impact.

And for good reason. They pursued and passionately completed many God-honoring tasks and missions. Their good works exemplified character and integrity. They labored intensively to serve one another, and they maintained a standard of righteousness they refused to lower in order to placate the culture around them. They held the truth in such high regard that they tested the words taught by so-called ministers to ensure that the doctrine they received did not malign or misconstrue it. They had persevered through much hardship and had remained faithful under pressure. And yet, after acknowledging their good works, Jesus in His message to this group of believers chastised them for one single heartrending deficiency: *they'd left their first love.* They were firing up the motor of religion without the disciple's fire of heartfelt passion for God.

How had this happened? Logic would say it made no sense. Their sacred zeal for God had deadened and diminished at the same time as their laundry list of good deeds had increased and intensified. But when our hearts are no longer glued to the Father's heart in a disciple's posture of grateful love and devotion, our motivation for doing even noble service to Him and to others becomes skewed and distorted.

Yes, the Ephesians were continuing to accomplish many good things, but He who knows the contents of the soul knew their hearts were no longer in it. Their commitment was not rooted as before in friendship with Him. It was no longer birthed out of an endearing passion. Christian living had become a chore for the Ephesians, reduced to a robotic "Can I help?" posture that lacked authenticity. They were effective but without affection.

Again, duty devoid of devotion.

And it caught the attention of God.

Consider how critical our love must be to Him that He would take time to point out its lack when writing a book as poignant as the Revelation is to Scripture. After all, this is the God of the universe we're talking about. He has the throes of the galaxy to control. He has the epochs of history to sovereignly orchestrate. He is keeping the planets aligned. He is keeping countries and continents stabilized. All while preparing for His return to earth. In other words, epic objectives are on His to-do list for today. And yet He addresses, of all things . . . love? To people He says are doing all the things they're supposed to be doing?

Why? Because more than all else, *love* is what He wants our relationship and our full surrender to be rooted in. Not just love, but *first* love—the only way we can serve Him for a lifetime. There is no other way for us to experience the true fulfillment of our "heart's desires" in life unless our chief "delight" is in Him alone.

Which is why this wake-up call to the love the Ephesian believers had "abandoned" was less an assignment to undertake (which they were obviously good at) and more of an invitation to accept. Even as it alerted them to the imbalance in their lifestyle and attitudes, it summoned them to come back to the position of friendship that He'd redeemed them to experience.

And maybe, just maybe, this chapter of our journey together is a wake-up call for you too. Maybe it's the first time in a long time you've considered in a deep, quiet, deliberate way the posture of your own heart. Maybe it's not occurred to you at this level of force that your effective Christian life is not a suitable replacement for an authentically passionate one. Maybe the people who follow you on social media are buying it but not the Lord. Not if it's done from anything else but love.

You and I can be impressive without intimacy.

Lord, help us.

I'll admit, again, in many seasons of my life, the Father has graciously alerted me to a callousness and indifference within me, even as my ministry was visibly growing. He has shown me where my heart was no longer pulsating with a brimming fervor that bubbled over into my attitudes and behaviors.

Few if any of the people around me would've known the gap that existed between my head and my heart because I was still fully capable of carrying out certain duties with a smile and charisma. I went to church on Sundays, read my Bible fairly regularly, and was diligent about serving others through our ministry. I even taught God's Word to many of them, participated in Christian events, and led my own sons in Scripture memorization.

Yet I often didn't even realize I was operating from a place of habit and obligation rather than passionate, enthusiastic fervor. I'd just grown so accustomed to the rhythm of *doing* that I'd neglected my state of *being*.

I *loved* Him. But not first. And maybe I could have been satisfied with that. But the Father could not. And so in one way or another—usually through the kind but stern counsel of a wise and godly mentor—He would bring His love for me to my attention, and show me that what He mainly desired from me was to experience my love for Him. Not my busyness but my love.

Jesus said it this way:

> "Love the Lord your God with all your heart, with all your soul, and with all your mind." This is the greatest and most important command. (Matt. 22:37–38)

How could I overlook something so simple yet so poignant while doing so much?

So on bended knee and with humility of heart, I would return to Him and ask Him to do what I could not seem to do for myself—to stoke the embers in my soul that seemed dull and lifeless. And I would ask my close friends and mentors to join me in praying that I would truly love the Lord with all my heart, soul, mind, and strength.

There may only be eighteen inches between the human head and the human heart, but it can be a long and arduous journey, migrating the contents of the first one to the second one. The Lord knows and understands our struggle. So along with the Ephesians of two millennia ago, hearing this personal letter from Jesus being read in their presence, let's sit here as disciples do, eager to listen and obey, and let our Lord give us the road map that will lead us back to a first love we've perhaps forgotten.

Remember

The first word of Revelation 2:5 is the first of three important steps that enable us to cooperate with the Holy Spirit in restoring our godly passion.

Remember.

Remember then how far you have fallen.

Jesus was speaking to Christians who were established and effective enough to rock the world they were living in, yet He encouraged them to pause, rest in nostalgia, and think back to those days when they were new at this, when their hearts were young, alive, and in love with Jesus.

Apparently, they'd grown out of it. In all their forward movement and activity, they'd sailed past the part where the extravagance of His love for them was a thought they just couldn't get over—His sacrifice for them, His willingness to come to them in their emptiness and shame, bringing to them the promise of a fresh, forgiven start in life. Where had that passion gone? They didn't know. Jesus was right. It wasn't the same as it had once been. But how could they start to recapture it?

Remember.

> Remember that at one time you were Gentiles in the flesh. . . . At that time you were without Christ, excluded from the citizenship of Israel, and foreigners to the covenants of promise, without hope and without God in the world. But now in Christ Jesus, you who were far away have been brought near by the blood of Christ. (Eph. 2:11–13)

Remember how you came to know Him. Remember the fervor you shared between you. Remember the disciplines that undergirded you, how you kept them not just on your calendar but in your heart, like your next meal, hungry for the fellowship. Remember what stirred you to follow Him in the first place, how your earthly reality shifted as excitedly as your eternal destiny, because of His grace at work in you.

There's great value in remembering.

When I was a little girl, one of my favorite TV programs was *Diff'rent Strokes*. It was a hilarious half-hour sitcom that followed two young inner-city kids—Arnold and Willis—who, after their mother died, had been adopted by a wealthy widower named Mr. Drummond. These boys had grown up impoverished, existing in circumstances that offered little provision for the present and little opportunity for the future. Their lives now, however, were the complete opposite. The Upper East Side home they shared with Mr. Drummond and his daughter was filled with all the regalia of wealth and affluence. The contrast between this new reality and their previous reality made for some good entertainment.

Throughout the series, the boys would often reflect on the life they'd previously known. They missed certain aspects of their upbringing, but each trip down memory lane resulted in a renewed sense of gratitude for what their adoptive parent had afforded them. Living here gave them a new perspective and outlook on life that would've escaped them if not for the generosity and kindness of this gentle benefactor. Even when they sometimes became disgruntled by his rules or frustrated by his standards, they'd soon remember what they'd been given, how many blessings had been deposited into their account, and they'd return with a rekindled sense of love and gratitude for him.

As believers, we can easily become so accustomed to the goodness and grace of God that we grow entitled and ungrateful, forgetting the depths from which we've been rescued, forgetting how dramatically our lives have shifted because of the sheer, unadulterated kindness of the Lord.

I've met and known many people who've told me riveting, supernatural testimonies that are unforgettable to hear. They were on the brink of suicide, their lives riddled with addictions that were tearing them and their loved ones apart. Others have said they had no sense of purpose at all, as if their lives were nothing more than a meaningless wandering from one twenty-four-hour period to another. Hopeless. Then they met Jesus, and the difference was incredible—more drastic than some others who, by His grace, were spared some of those unthinkable circumstances.

But even in these types of cases, the passing of time can begin to dull the difference. Even these lives, rescued from such debilitating pasts, can devolve into a present monotonous rhythm of tradition and habit. If we're not careful about intentionally recalling the death trap we've all been rescued from and the divine relationship we've all been graciously adopted into, we will become lulled into a spiritual sleep. All of us.

Before Christ, we were "dead" in our "trespasses and sins." We were held captive to "fleshly desires, carrying out the inclinations of our flesh and thoughts, and we were by nature children under wrath." Our plight was bleak. The outlook for our future was grim. "But God, who is rich in mercy, because of his great love that he had for us, made us alive with Christ even though we were dead in trespasses" (Eph. 2:1–5). He did that for us. Can you believe it? You *have* believed it. But do you feel it? Do you love Him for it, the way you once loved Him for it?

Remember.

One of the spiritual disciplines that most effectively supports this habit of remembering for me has been journaling. When I started doing it in my teenage years, I had no idea how crucial it would become in cultivating and nourishing my passion for the Lord. I'm not as consistent at it as I should be. And I'm not one of those detailed people who carefully denotes the happenings of each day with brilliant prose and sharp precision. But God has helped me keep a general account of His activity in my life through the years, and those writings have become for me a track record of His constant presence with me. Often when I'm discouraged or uncertain, I'll go back to some of those books, to moments I would otherwise have forgotten. But there they are. Firsthand comments, fresh from the action, and yet so often exactly what I needed to remember today. The Lord knew I'd need to remember— *the Lord knows we need to remember!*—and He's provided us pathways for remembering His faithfulness, to stoke again the passion in our souls.

So think back. Where would you be if God had not initiated relationship with you? To what depths might you have fallen if not for the restraining power of His Spirit who lives within you? What kind of hopeless future might you be looking toward if Christ hadn't come from heaven to earth, living and dying and living again so that your life, even with its problems, could be filled with His promises? And what track record of miracles and open doors has He provided for you throughout the different seasons and stages of your life?

God has been faithful. Pause and remember.

Repent

The second instruction John gave to the Ephesian believers who'd been low on their first love for Christ was "repent" (Rev. 2:5). *Repent* is a word that has lost its weightiness through the years. It's rarely mentioned plainly anymore, having been replaced by far more palatable alternatives like "apologize" or "regret." The same watering-down is true for terms like *sin* and *holiness* too. Their importance and impact have been minimized in order to stave off any alarm about the cost associated with them. Better advertising. Better public relations.

But much of the distance we often feel in our relationship with Jesus, much of the lack of authentic spiritual fervor we experience in trying to serve Him, finds its source in this less-than-clear understanding of what *repentance* really means and what it really looks like to pursue it.

Sugarcoating it may have gotten us through the day sometimes and helped us sleep better at night, but it hasn't helped us to grow in spiritual maturity. And it's diminished the high view of God's standard that Scripture gives us, thereby cheapening the value we place on loving Him. It's weakened us by convincing us that God has lowered His standard of holiness to accommodate our failings, when in actuality God *in His love* has kept His Word consistent, knowing that only by obeying Him—which we can only do from genuine affection—can we experience His fullness.

So for those of us who desire to pursue true discipleship, we must come face-to-face with the hard-hitting, sharpshooting reality of repentance. It's not a feeling; it's an action. Repentance means to turn from going one way and intentionally go another. It's a *change* in direction.

In confession we acknowledge the areas where we've fallen short of God's glory in our attitudes and actions, but if we stop there—with admittance—we haven't completed the cycle of repentance. To be sure, "If we confess our sins, he is faithful and righteous to forgive us our sins and to cleanse us from all unrighteousness" (1 John 1:9). Very true. We bank on that hope. But until confession, spurred on by a godly sorrow, turns the corner to repentance (2 Cor. 7:10)—until it moves beyond words and intentions into a real, repentant change of direction—Christ cannot be our first love. Something or someone else is. And as much as we don't want to let go of it, this something is chaining us down. It is fighting our freedom. There is no going forward to a steadily fulfilling life of sincerity and strength until that sin is quickly getting smaller in our rearview mirror.

Think about the last time you were driving somewhere and realized you were going in the wrong direction, getting farther away from your destination, not closer. Simply acknowledging to yourself, or to the other people in your car, that you'd made a mistake couldn't solve your situation. *Confession* is only the start of a process. And if confession is where the process ends, there's no point to the process at all.

The goal of awareness and admittance is to *change direction*. You get off at the next ramp. You turn back against the flow of traffic. You point your hood where your trunk used to be. You speed off the other way.

Otherwise, it doesn't matter. Otherwise, nothing changes.

Making the turn might feel embarrassing at first, especially if you have passengers with you. It almost

certainly won't be easy to make all the corrective maneu-
vers required to change course. But until you trust the
same Spirit who enlightens and enables your confession
to empower your repentance—to turn you around and
get you on the right track—the feeling will never catch up
to the performance. You'll just be fueling a fruitless trip.
What a waste.

To someone who desires spiritual fervor and intimacy
in their relationship with the Lord, repentance is key
because sin will just continue to "cut you off from God"
(Isa. 59:2 NLT). It's not as though you lose your standing
as His child, but you can lose your intimacy with Him.
Your level of rest and comfort with Him, of peace and
contentment, can plummet because He is holy and cannot
relate to unholiness.

Many believers often govern themselves, their choices,
and their behaviors by teasing themselves with this question: "How close can I get to sin without crossing the
line?" But the disciple who is pursuing a "first love" relationship with a holy God is asking something entirely
different. She is asking, "How close can I get to Jesus?"
Proximity to sin is not her concern; proximity to Jesus is.

So she doesn't toy with the line of sin. Instead, she
governs her choices based on what will draw her closest to
her Savior and conform her into His image. Her compass
for living is articulated in the following words, commonly
attributed to Susanna Wesley in the 1700s . . .

> Whatever weakens your reason, impairs the tenderness of your conscience, obscures your sense of God, takes off your relish for spiritual things, whatever increases the authority of the body over the mind, that thing is sin to you, however innocent it may seem in itself.

Go back, dear reader, and meditate on that statement again, being careful to digest its layers. What are the hobbies and habits, the liberties and lifestyle choices that are dulling your spiritual senses or quieting the conviction of God's Spirit within you? Are there any things that, even if not sinful in essence, are taking the position of first place in your life, giving your flesh mastery over your spirit? If so, these things are sin for you. Because you are His disciple, and He must be first. Above all else. Sole master and king.

Repent.

Lay that thing down.

Move it back into its rightful position of being subject to the Savior.

Yahweh is our eternal, unchanging, loving heavenly Father. He never moves; He never shifts. He is always present with us, eager to relate to us and engage with us as His sons and daughters. So whenever our relationship with Him feels like a dutiful connection between distant associates, we are the ones, not Him, who've created the distance. Sin or weighty hindrances have wedged a gap in there. And don't we know from long trying, we do not own a crowbar strong enough to shove those sins and indulgences out. Even if temporarily dislodged, they keep coming back.

Except when we restore Him to the place where He belongs. *First* place. Then amazingly, there's just no more room in the car for them anymore. And even if we could fit them, we don't want them anymore. We've fixed our love on Jesus now, the way a surrendered disciple does it. Repenting. Changing direction. And the way we see it, all we want from now on is to stay on this road for good.

Repeat

After *remembering*, after *repenting*, the final instruction from Jesus for John to give to the Ephesians was to *repeat*.

Remember then how far you've fallen; repent, and *do the works you did at first*. (Rev. 2:5, emphasis added)

Earlier, I let you in on the beginning of Jerry's and my romantic relationship. Like any couple genuinely endeared to each other, we prioritized each other above everyone else. Even the simplest activities became valuable and desirable, full of expectation and excitement. Couples in love can hardly do anything else but think about the other one. They rearrange their schedules around their times together. When they talk, it's almost never forced or awkward. They're increasingly vulnerable with each other. They share their deepest joys and sorrows, things that perhaps no one else even knows. They listen—they *really listen*—not for the purpose of correcting but with a genuine desire to understand and get to know their beloved, to solidify and cultivate their growing intimacy. They count the other person's interests as being worth the time to pursue because of how eagerly they want to please this one they care so much about.

Then they get married.

They've joined their lives together now in the most intimate of ways, and yet the tendency from here on is to let many of the fundamentals that drew them together go by the wayside. Life is busy with details and decisions, with work schedules and conflicting assumptions, and before they know it, it's like they're sleeping next to a stranger. They don't feel the same attraction they once did. Instead of continuing to learn each other, they've learned to go through the motions of relationship without the joy that used to be attached to it.

It's common. It's natural. It happens. We know it. But central to why it occurs so often is because couples neglect many of the activities they once did as a matter of course. They don't spend time together like they used to do. They don't talk with each other as honestly as they once did. They don't listen the same way, generously and attentively. They don't consider the other's opinion before making unilateral decisions. They don't treat the other person as if their joy is their driving pursuit.

As a result, spouses share the same home, the same bed, and the same last name but have no passion.

They're not in "first love" anymore.

But the things we know about regaining intimacy in human relationships are much the same as what's required to regain it in our friendship with Jesus. We need to *repeat* the things we did at first.

Remember? That's part of it, remembering. But then do it. *Repeat it.* Sounds crazy, maybe, but see what it stirs up if you really did.

How did you once prioritize your time in His love letter to you, the Bible? How often did you read it? How did you savor it? What did you do to help yourself keep it in mind and think about it through the day?

How did you talk to Him in prayer? When and where did you pray? While you were driving? While you were washing the dishes? While you were working out on the treadmill? While you were cutting the grass or drying your hair?

How did you worship Him? Only on Sundays? Only at church? Or did you keep praise music wafting through the house and through your earbuds throughout each day? Did you literally get down on your knees when you tried to express to Him how you felt about Him? Did you lift your hands? Did you care who heard or saw you?

How did you talk about Him to others? Did He come up easily in conversation? Were you eager to tell people what He could do, what He'd done for you? When people asked if you would pray for them, did you stop right then and pray with them right there? Remember how it felt?

You did it *then*. His interests were your interests. His plans were your plans. His Word was your command. Remember? Then repeat it. Do it now.

And see if love doesn't find you again.

I've seen a don't-notice-me nod of indifference walk through my door and into my house before. I've heard a dry, moody, obligatory voice say something that sounded like "How can I help you?" without giving off a whiff of true, heartfelt affection or gratitude. Worse, I've seen and heard the same thing in my own posture and tone of voice as well, even knowing this body I inhabit has been transformed by God's power and grace into a sanctuary, a holy house, for the Holy Spirit.

I'm tired of duty without devotion. Believing without discipleship. I'd love to be different, wouldn't you?

Well then, let's get to it.

We know what to do first.

Surrendering All

I pray this: that your love will keep on growing in
knowledge and every kind of discernment.
Philippians 1:9

Consider the way you invest your time and treasures. What does this reveal about what or who has first place in your life?

_____

_____

_____

_____

_____

_____

_____

_____

_____

_____

Go back to page 155 and prayerfully consider Susanna Wesley's statement. Ask the Holy Spirit to reveal anything in your life that falls within one of the categories she points out.

_____

_____

_____

_____

_____

_____

_____

_____

_____

_____

_____

_____

_____

In seasons of your life when you may have felt an absence of authentic desire to honor the Lord, how have you seen either emotionalism or legalism sneak into your spiritual life? Are either of these something that you are dealing with now? If so, how is the Lord calling you to release them to Him?

_____

_____

_____

_____

_____

_____

_____

_____

_____

_____

_____

For Further Reading

Psalm 27:4 • Matthew 6:33 • Matthew 22:37

CHAPTER 6

Everything You Face

My goal is to know him and the power of his
resurrection and the fellowship of his sufferings.
Philippians 3:10

We recently had the honor of introducing a beautiful woman named Michelle to the members of my home church in Dallas. For more than twenty years, she's been one of the leaders in Bible Study Fellowship (BSF), an organization that conducts high-quality, in-depth Bible study experiences for people in communities all over the world.

Michelle, who's taught these small-group studies to women of every race, background, and generation, has made the study and communication of God's Word the central focus of her life and ministry to others. My own sister, Chrystal, was one of her students and always raved about Michelle's keen insight, clarity, and compelling ability to reveal the Scriptures and make them come alive.

She has a vibrancy you can see and feel when you're around her in any setting. Her personality is bright and bubbly. Her beautiful eyes seem to penetrate your soul when she's speaking to you. Her robust laugh is simply contagious. But all this beaming charisma could easily distract a person from noticing one unique characteristic about Michelle.

She is almost completely blind.

On the day we invited her to our church to receive a financial gift for BSF, a member of our hospitality team escorted her across the large platform to the center of the stage. But anyone seeing her for the first time would've assumed we were just being extra attentive and helpful to our guest, maybe to calm her nerves at being in front of so many people. She wore that same electrifying smile on her face, interlacing her arm with that of her attendant, like two friends who just loved being together. Not until my sister, greeting her at the microphone, mentioned Michelle's fifty-year struggle with her eyesight did anyone else in the room probably even suspect.

Among the most memorable things I remember Chrystal recounting that day was something she recalled Michelle saying during one of her classes. She'd explained that while her loss of vision was an ailment she never would've chosen, it had produced for her an undeniably invaluable benefit. Losing her physical vision had heightened her spiritual vision. Not being able to see had given

her the ability to see life, truth, God, and others in an
entirely different way. As her physical eyes had dimmed,
her spiritual eyes had seemed to open more and more.

Blindness had given her sight.

Undistracted by normal visual stimuli, she'd become
more perceptive and sensitive to the guidance of the
Holy Spirit. In not having to deal with all the competing
offerings a sighted person can entertain, she and others
in similar circumstances develop the capacity to discern
things others cannot. Invisible realities take center stage.
Michelle said she could sense more deeply now the heart
of God, could view in higher definition the purposes of
God, could tune in more clearly to hear the voice of God.

She never wished to be blind, of course. But a surrendered disciple is the first to notice value in adversity. They
are the first to grasp how hardship and difficulty come
with a corresponding fellowship and intimacy with the
Lord that no other experience can deliver—the fellowship
and intimacy with Him that we were created to enjoy.

௸

> But whatever things were gain to me, these
> things I have counted as loss because of
> Christ. More than that, I count all things
> to be loss in view of the surpassing value of
> knowing Christ Jesus my Lord, for whom

I have suffered the loss of all things, and
count them mere rubbish, so that I may gain
Christ . . . that I may know Him and the
power of His resurrection and the fellowship
of His sufferings, being conformed to His
death. (Phil. 3:7–8, 10 NASB)

These verses are some of the most well-loved and
recognizable in the New Testament. When quoting them,
we applaud Paul's all-in dedication to Christ. How could
he still write like this? After being reviled and ridiculed.
After being imprisoned and beaten. After enduring so
much mistreatment at the hands of others for refusing to
back down from his sacred commitment.

Paul was a follower undeterred by difficulty, undistracted by accolades, unashamed of the gospel, and
unfazed by the pressure of his peers. Despite all his pain-
ful losses, he could declare with clear-eyed determination
his one holy ambition: to be intimately allied with Christ.

To know Him. That's what we want too, isn't it? We
can get on board with that. You and I as disciples of
Christ want to know His purposes and His ways. It's
probably what drew you to this book in the first place—to
know Him—to know Him and, as Paul said, to know *His
resurrection power.*

Back in Ephesians 1, where that foundational description of our Christian identity is found, the Bible says the

"immeasurable greatness of his power toward us who believe" is the same power that God exercised in Christ "by raising him from the dead" (Eph. 1:19–20). The same! That's what's available to us now—this same level of holy power. We want His power emboldening us to live as the overcomers we've been saved to become.

Yet even as we feel our spiritual burners igniting when we read of Paul's fervor, when our hearts echo with his desires, longing to mirror them, Paul interjects something else that stings us and dampens our initial enthusiasm. His goal, he said, is "that I may know Him and the power of His resurrection and . . .

"the fellowship of his sufferings."

Okay, the "fellowship" part, of course, is a desirable goal of ours, like knowing Him, like knowing His resurrection power. But should "sufferings" really appear on this same list? On the same line? Side by side with fellowship? Because, honestly, we've got difficulties right now we wish would go away. We've got hardships we'd much rather avoid than experience. We've got adversities we'd give almost anything to circumvent.

But what if they are the dynamics that will invite us and usher us into a deeper union with our Savior? What if there is a communion and depth of friendship with Jesus that only comes to those who've held His hand and walked with Him through seasons of suffering?

Because those seasons are coming. We most certainly do not have to seek them. When they come, it doesn't mean we're more godly than others now that we're going through hardship, any more than we should think we're more godly than others when we are enjoying seasons of ease and comfort. But difficulty, in some form or fashion, will eventually find us. The world in which we live will never fail to bring hardship to our doorstep. *Existing* is the only prerequisite for *experiencing* it. We are, after all, inhabitants of a planet where evil prevails and where everything else besides our souls, our God, and His everlasting kingdom is temporary in nature. All the rest of it decays and crumbles and shows signs of weakening and wear.

Even a newly built house will eventually need its roof replaced. Even our brand-new clothes will be stained and one day begin to unravel. Even a newborn baby, as strange as it sounds, starts the clock on the aging process as soon as she emerges from the womb. Though powdery fresh and new at birth, she is already on her way to becoming a teenager whose face is oily and blemished, a middle-aged woman whose joints are stiff and tender, an older woman whose skin is wrinkling and her hair is turning gray. This is the natural order of the earth. Aging. Changing. Hardening. Slowing.

And while certain aspects of getting older bring pleasant benefits and blessings in their wake, like the comfortable hominess of a mature house or the wisdom of an elder's years, they also contain expanded opportunities for all-new difficulties to crop up. Failures. Fading abilities. Sickness. Sorrows.

And yet . . .

God in His grace and mercy infuses purpose into these inevitabilities. He sovereignly keeps these hard realities from becoming a wasted wilderness. He allows and uses adversity to boost our capacity for detecting and digesting what matters most in life. Instead of leaving us buried under the sadness, frustration, and uneasiness we feel, he leverages our disappointment to remind us, "This world is not our permanent home" (Heb. 13:14 NLT). When measured in His capable hands, they whet our appetite for things eternal.

Something inside us knows—*we just know*—we were made for something different from sadness and suffering. Something more. Something eternal. We've been reborn for a reality that doesn't include death, separation, divorce, and decline. That's why we are so jarred and wracked with grief when they occur. The transforming task of hardship, then, is to keep us from becoming too attached to the things of this earth. It loosens this grip of ours that is far too prone to hold on too tightly to other things, other people, and other blessings than the priceless blessing of knowing Jesus our Savior, Jesus our Lord.

Difficulty, like nothing else, points us to Him.

It is uniquely able to make us more like Him.

Still, for people like us, who value the ease and lightness of comfort, this cost of communion is asking a lot. But if we're serious about wanting to "know Him," if we're serious about wanting to experience the "power of His resurrection" in everyday life, we need to heed what our newly opened spiritual eyes are showing us.

Comfort *itself* is in no way wrong or less godly. But it doesn't demand much of us in the way of character and maturity. Instead, it has a way of making us complacent and entitled. It makes us expect nothing different from day to day than our cherished peace and quiet, or our cherished activities and amusements, and then to feel deprived and resentful if these things are not made available to us.

But it is so hard to desire and depend on Jesus from the cradle of comfort. It takes so much more effort to press into Him when we have nothing pressing against us. One of the main catalysts of walking with a devoted, hungry heart for God is for the sunshine of our comfort to be interrupted by a rainstorm of difficulty. Only then, it seems, are we ever jolted into a real remembrance that *life* is not our life. *Jesus* is our life.

Look back on your own experience and think about the lives of others whose walk with Christ you most admire. You'll find that in many cases adversity has been the most effective way of raising your (and their) spiritual alert level, turning your focus so sharply toward Him that you couldn't

take your eyes off Him. These seasons have been a cata-
lyst in maintaining a seriousness for toning your spiritual
muscles, because you urgently needed to be certain that
they'd be strong enough to keep you standing the next day.

In times of pain and uncertainty, we long to hear
Him. We search for Him and His will in His Word with
a fervor and eagerness that wasn't there on easier days.
In desperation, we prostrate our hearts and bodies before
Him, knowing that the miracle we need is beyond the
reach of our on-hand resources. We walk through each
day in nearly nonstop prayer, our spiritual senses tuned to
see what God might be working to accomplish in those
invisible realities that surround our difficult visible ones.

Our heart wasn't here until we touched rock bottom.
But in sensing ourselves sinking into situations that were
so far over our heads, we finally grip a truth in our heart
that we once only theorized in our heads: He is the Rock
at the bottom. And He's been here all along—here, there,
and everywhere in between. We no longer merely believe
it by faith. We know it by experience. So we surrender all
to Him. Even this. Even now.

We are finally coming to know Him.

∽

I want you to pause with me for a moment because,
while I don't know the specific things you suffer with,

while I don't know the exact fears and struggles that send you reaching out hard for God, I do know they're significant, and I am not minimizing their weight in your life. I mean that. Yet in nearly every way, troubles of this kind are common to every person, different only by the degree and the details. We spend our lives trying to skirt around them and heal from them, and we hope the next one isn't coming anytime soon. It's what *I* do, it's what *you* do, it's what we *all* do.

But Paul, in this Philippians 3 summary statement of his goals in life, which includes his desire to participate in a difficult "fellowship" with Christ, points to a suffering even more precise than just the natural suffering that accompanies the human condition. Read closely and you'll recognize it: "the fellowship of *his* sufferings" (v. 10)—of Christ's suffering—a type of suffering specific to our Lord and, to hear Paul say it, a type of suffering specific also to the disciple.

It's called *persecution*—the hardship we experience because of our allegiance to Christ, the suffering we endure because we've "taken up our cross" to follow Him. Within this necessary suffering lies a more unique communion with Jesus than that of health scares and job loss and all the other maladies and misfortunes of humanity. To suffer for Christ is to experience a level of crisis and difficulty that is specifically correlated to our unreserved and unshakable devotion to Jesus. If we, as disciples, are fully committed followers of Christ, unashamed of Him, wholehearted in our loyalty to Him, we *will* experience a suffering that accompanies our unabandoned allegiance to Him.

It will be unavoidable. And it will be ugly.

In his classic book on discipleship, German pastor and martyr Dietrich Bonhoeffer described the suffering of Jesus on the cross. His suffering was compounded, he said, by including not only His palpable pain but also His public rejection, which "removed all dignity and honor from his suffering."[2] Without rejection, some suffering can be considered dignified. Christ's suffering was humiliating. He went to the cross not as an admired martyr but as a scorned and taunted criminal. Ridiculed and belittled. Ostracized by the powers of His day, even denied by His companions, betrayed by a close friend.

His was an ugly suffering.

And His suffering was specifically tied to His deity. He went to the cross precisely because He was Christ and King. His suffering was intertwined with His mission as our Redeemer and His assignment as our Savior. And just as His cross and the rejection that accompanied it were specific to His sacred mission, our suffering will be specific to our identity as His followers.

Yes, dear friend, we *follow* Him into this fellowship of suffering.

To the extent we are surrendered to Jesus—unashamed
of our dedication to Him in every area of life—to this
extent we will be increasingly marginalized by society.
And even, I daresay, by some sectors of the church and
the Christian culture of modern times. I'm not talking
about being marginalized for being rude and obnoxious
to others, illegitimately offensive, condescending, or
intentionally confrontational. But as we become more
Christlike in our convictions and our presentation, delivering them in love, grace, and wisdom, we will swing in
the opposite direction of norms that our society tolerates
and promotes. We will contrast with the behaviors and
beliefs that current culture accentuates as being acceptable. The result will be an ever-widening gap and a
noticeably uncomfortable marginalization from others.

In other words, disciples should expect disapproval.

Like Jesus did.

Yes, *expect* it, my fellow disciple. Anticipate it. As
"strangers and exiles" in this world (1 Pet. 2:11), we must
prepare ourselves to endure it on some level. We've been
called to stand out from those who line our streets and
cities, as well as those who line our pews but only pretend
to be serious about being His followers. We will not go
unnoticed if we truly live our faith. "In fact, all who want
to live a godly life in Christ Jesus will be persecuted"
(2 Tim. 3:12). It will hurt. It will cost.

We will suffer.

I've become much more aware and sensitive to this reality the older I've become—not mostly because of its impact on *me* (there's that, too) but because of its increasingly escalating impact on my children.

At the time of this writing, as I've already said, my sons are twenty-one, nineteen, and fifteen. They're in the glorious stages of blossoming adulthood, where they're finding their footing in careers and purpose and where their faith is becoming more personal and practical.

When they were young, I taught them Scripture. We'd memorize tiny portions of it, layer by layer, until it became whole verses and then chapters. Since we home-schooled them for a few years, I had the luxury of incorporating this routine into their curriculum. In addition to that, we took them to a healthy church where they met like-minded people and learned how to serve the body of Christ. We had many discussions about spiritual things and how to relate them to the world around us. I look back on so many times when we'd be sitting around the breakfast table or getting ready for bed at night—all the opportunities we took to impress on them the values and implications of being a follower of Christ, in ways that aligned with their maturity levels at each stage of childhood. Our parenting was far from perfect. In hindsight, I'd do many things differently. But I can say, with much gratitude to my husband, that Jerry and I have genuinely tried to be intentional about their spiritual formation.

We also tried to raise them to feel secure in their manhood. Most every day of their lives, I reminded them of who they were called to be, in words I strung together from biblical truth and said to them out loud:

> You are men of integrity, character, and honesty who will love God with all of your heart and soul and strength. You are a leader. You are not a follower. You are the head. You are not the tail. You are above. You are not beneath. You are humble, kind, generous, and strong. You were not made to fit in with the crowd. You are different. Today, you will be a blessing to your teachers, your brothers, and your friends. And you will remember that you can do all things through Christ who gives you strength.

My sons can still repeat these lines verbatim because they heard them almost every morning of their upbringing. I said it to them over and over in hopes it would become the soundtrack of their behaviors and attitudes. I prayed that when they'd grow up to make their own decisions, choose their own relationships, and exhibit their own character, it would align with these truths. Even now as they move nearer to and into their twenties, I still text it to them regularly when we're apart, and I say it to them out loud when we're together.

Feel free to steal those words if you like for your children and grandchildren.

But here's what I know. They are coming of age in a world that is mostly antithetical to what their father and I have taught them and from what the Scriptures have shown them.

If my boys choose, and I pray they will, to rise up as men whose daily lives mirror biblical values and reflect a surrendered devotion to Christ, they will automatically become outsiders in many circles.

If they honor God's design for manhood; if they value and defer to authority; if they respect and honor women; if they choose to speak the truth in love regarding marriage, sexuality, and gender; if they refuse promiscuity and practice monogamy to one wife; if they build promising careers without compromising their integrity or disregarding others to accomplish it, they will find themselves out of step with the self-focused, live-your-own-truth, self-promoting, salacious, hustle-and-grind ethics of their post-Christian era.

But that's just the start.

If they choose to do all these things unashamedly for the glory of the one true God; if they freely share their faith and lead others to Jesus; if they are boldly consistent in the biblical standards they maintain as young men, young husbands, and young parents themselves; and if in pursuing lives of humility, selflessness, and godly restraint they outspokenly deflect all praise to their Lord and Savior, they will be persecuted. They will be ridiculed. Discarded and discredited. Despised and rejected. Their "friends" will look at them strangely, stop inviting them to hang out, talk about them behind their backs, and enlist others to do the same. They'll be cancelled on social media and passed over for opportunities where the powers that be would rather employ people whose convictions are less concrete, substantial, and politically incorrect.

They will experience a disciple's pain, these sons of mine, these sons and daughters of yours, our grandsons and our granddaughters. And so will we. It will require backbone because it will be hard for us as well. We will suffer for following Jesus this closely, this devotedly, this comprehensively. For surrendering all.

And though it will not be without the burden of loss and exclusion, it will also not be without the blessing of "fellowship."

". . . the fellowship of his sufferings."

〜

One of my favorite books is *Jesus Freaks*, a book that eventually became a several-volume series, published by an organization called Voice of the Martyrs. This ministry seeks to bring awareness to the plights of people who are being persecuted, abused, imprisoned, even killed for their faith in Christ in countries where believers face continual threats against themselves and their families.

These books tell many of their stories, happening even today, as well as stories of saints in centuries past who paid horrible costs for refusing to deny their Savior. In every entry I've ever read, I can barely digest some of the suffering that so many people, both older and younger, have undergone against state-sponsored security forces and rogue militia gangs, just because they're disciples of Jesus.

Some of them have been blackballed from whole industries, leaving them without a stream of revenue to support their families. Teenagers have been kicked out of their homes and left to fend for themselves on the street after being caught reading a copy of the Scriptures by flashlight in the dark corners of their home. Parents have been arrested and stripped from their children, who've then been shuffled into the revolving door of a broken government system. Students have been bullied, backed against a wall of ridicule and rejection. Worse yet, there are stories of how a lifetime of possessions were burned to the ground, how loved ones were kidnapped, how bones were broken. In many cases, of course, their very lives were taken from them.

And yet what continues to rivet me every time I read these stories is the steadied peace these people described experiencing, despite the devastating pain and losses they faced. They tell of a joy that anchors them securely, a sense of the Spirit's nearness and oversight. They recount clear dreams and visions where God assured them of His presence and of their deepening hunger to hear His voice through the scraps of Scripture they were able to smuggle into their prison cells.

Do you hear that? It's the sound of futures being wrecked, fingers being cracked, children screaming for their parents, hollow moans echoing in the night. Yet above it, inside it, and all around it, you hear of a deep thirst for God being heightened, people's passionate pursuit of Him becoming intensified, their desire for heaven being renewed into living hope, and a level of communication with Christ that's as real and tangible as the hand in front of their face. His Word on their breath. His abundant life beating illogically in their hearts.

His nearness, like a fellowship.

For most of us, the ways in which we'll experience persecution for our faith will pale in comparison to these examples I've given. We'll likely never be arrested, starved, or martyred for the sake of Christ. But while our physical bodies may not be burned at a stake, our pride will need to be if we will even begin to endure the relatively minor cost of being ignored, replaced, marginalized, rejected, discredited, or overlooked. We must receive whatever form of faith-based suffering comes our way, viewing it not as a full stop to all our hopes and plans but as a runway into a season of deeper intimacy with Jesus than we've ever known.

It won't be easy. It won't be fun. It may even, at times, be nearly unbearable—being labeled as intolerant and small-minded, being looked upon as strange and unusual, being cancelled, unfollowed, and publicly berated. I've experienced all those things. I know how it feels.

But we are not alone. As God said to Elijah, after His weary prophet felt himself isolated to the point of being suicidal because of his many experiences of rejection and denigration, there were still as many as "seven thousand" faceless others scattered throughout Israel who hadn't bowed their knee to the false gods of the day (1 Kings 19:18). Even on his worst day, Elijah was still in good company.

And so are we—not only in fellowship with our fellow disciples but in a holy and sweet fellowship with Christ that sanctifies us, forges us, fashions us, detaches us from our enticing idols, and reorients our heart to love what He loves, to give importance to the things He knows are most important. Our increases in suffering for Him have been translated into an increased friendship with Him.

༺ఞ

Some of my most intimate friendships with other women have been cemented in the valley of dark times. It's possible your experience is much the same. When I think about the few lifelong friendships I most treasure, it's almost ironic how much the depth of our relationship is tied to the hard things we've walked through together.

Of course, we've shared a lot of levity along the way as well—many cups of coffee, many carefree outings, even some leisure trips to fun places where we've grown closer to each other by sharing good experiences. But the moments that have glued our hearts together into one heart have been those heavy hours of holding hands and holding each other when a parent died, when a miscarriage shattered our hopes, when a surgery brought all our fears to the surface, when an unfulfilled dream threatened to discourage the daylights out of us. These vulnerable moments broke through any of the shallowness that existed in our friendship, in our familiar banter, as we stepped into that space of hardship with one another and walked through tears to the other shore, where we were initiated into a new kind of friendship and fellowship.

There was a heightened compassion for each other. An awareness of the other's plight. A new interest in hearing from the Lord, wanting to bring the Father's perspective into all the things that were happening. A hunger for words to say or even just a silent shoulder to hug.

And here's what it took me a long time to realize: when our fellowship of suffering matures into the fellowship of *His* suffering, we stop focusing our prayers so much on asking Him to change the situations we're dealing with. Instead, we start asking Him how He wants to change us while we're in them. Instead of only asking why and being angry that He doesn't answer the way we want, we start asking *how—Lord, how can You get the most glory out of me, out of us, through this situation?* As one of my favorite authors of old, Elisabeth Elliot, said, "The secret is 'Christ in me,' not me in a different set of circumstances."[3] (See Col. 1:17.)

This is the disciple's passion.

Not to, first, be spared of suffering but to become formed into the image of Jesus through the suffering.

Listen, friend, He knows. He knows how it feels to suffer, in ways we'll never know. He sympathizes with us in our struggle because He's been here before, wanting the cup of anguish to pass from Him so that He wouldn't be required to drink its contents, and yet, "for the joy that lay before him, he endured the cross, despising the shame" (Heb. 12:2).

He now waits for us and intercedes for us, promising He will never leave us or forsake us as we walk down our long, lonely paths of suffering—both the suffering of this age and the suffering of Christian devotion. He has promised to receive in His heart each pang we feel, easing it, walking with us through it, and using it to draw us closer into His arms to experience a fellowship with Him we would otherwise never know.

Ask Michelle. She'll tell you.

In her not seeing, she's learned to see in an entirely different way.

Oh, my sister—oh, my brother—if you find yourself in the grip of suffering today, grab hold of your Savior more tightly than the pain has grabbed hold of you.

And don't let go.

Not now.

Not yet.

And not until you can say: "I had only heard about you before, but now I have seen you with my own eyes" (Job 42:5 NLT).

Surrendering All

Who can separate us from the love of Christ?
Can affliction or distress or persecution or famine
or nakedness or danger or sword?
Romans 8:35

Write about the most difficult circumstance you are facing right now. Answering honestly, is this experience
causing your heart to harden against God or is it drawing
you toward Him?

_____

_____

_____

_____

_____

_____

_____

_____

_____

In what ways have you seen certain streams of Christian community either (1) glamorize suffering as a mark of godliness or (2) glamorize ease and comfort as a mark of godliness?

_____

_____

_____

_____

_____

_____

_____

_____

_____

_____

_____

_____

_____

_____

Is there any way (or ways) in which a hardship you are experiencing now is specifically tied to your unapologetic faith in Jesus? On your job? In your family? Somewhere else? How is this suffering increasing your fellowship with the Lord?

_____

_____

_____

_____

_____

_____

_____

_____

_____

_____

_____

_____

For Further Reading

Matthew 5:11 • Philippians 3:8 • Hebrews 5:8

CHAPTER 7

Everywhere You Go

"Go, therefore, and make disciples of all nations,
baptizing them in the name of the Father
and of the Son and of the Holy Spirit."
Matthew 28:19

C. S. Lewis is one of my all-time favorite authors, and his book *Mere Christianity* is a classic. The last statements of his writing in this book speak the language of true disciples.

> Nothing that you have not given away will ever be really yours. Nothing in you that has not died will ever be raised from the dead. Look for yourself, and you will find in the long run only hatred, loneliness, despair, rage, ruin, and decay. But look for Christ and you will find Him, and with Him everything else thrown in.[4]

As we've traveled along together this far, I hope and pray that the call of Christ to *surrender all* has become your new rallying cry. It's become that for me. It requires some hard looks inside—probably with some painfully honest help from others—to root out the ground-in bastions of sin and self that resist being displaced for discipleship. Above all, it takes the searchlight of the Holy Spirit to find the less overt ones that hide and lurk in secret places.

And though much of what goes into making us the kind of disciples who are fully surrendered happens in those secret, personal spaces where no one else is looking—purposefully out of the public eye—discipleship is not entirely a private exercise. If it is only pursued in our prayer closets and through our personal spiritual disciplines, we will bump up against a built-in ceiling. Because, as C. S. Lewis put it plainly . . .

Nothing that you have not given away will ever be really yours.[5]

Maybe the next step you need in order to thrive as a devoted disciple is less private and more public in nature. Maybe the fulfillment you seek is found in giving away what you've been given. In completing the cycle of discipleship mentioned by Jesus in Matthew 28:19. In joining your disciple's heart with others. In taking your surrendered life out of the classroom and sharing what you've learned from God and from His Word with someone else.

"Go . . . and make disciples."

In one of His final conversations with the disciples before His crucifixion, Jesus said, "I still have many things to tell you, but you can't bear them now" (John 16:12). But on the other side of His death, He could share some of them. And His disciples could now know from visible experience, having seen Him come back to life from the grave, that He really *did* have the power to promise and predict all those things He'd promised and predicted for them along the way.

- "What is impossible with man is possible with God." (Luke 18:27)
- "Anything you ask the Father in my name, he will give you." (John 16:23)
- "When the Counselor comes, the one I will send to you from my Father . . . he will testify about me. You also will testify, because you have been with me from the beginning." (John 15:26–27)
- "Whenever they bring you before synagogues and rulers and authorities, don't worry about how you should defend yourself or what you should say. For the Holy Spirit will teach you at that very hour what must be said." (Luke 12:11–12)

When the disciples stood with Jesus for the last time on earth, before He ascended into heaven, He gave them His final words of command—the last of those "many things" He'd been waiting to tell them until after He'd risen from the dead.

> "Go, therefore, and make disciples of all nations, baptizing them in the name of the Father and of the Son and of the Holy Spirit, teaching them to observe everything I have commanded you. And remember, I am with you always, to the end of the age." (Matt. 28:19–20)

In the moment, the disciples didn't know how they were possibly going to accomplish this assignment. Despite the recharged renewal of faith they undoubtedly felt, they would have still wondered how they could possibly reach "all nations." This would have seemed like a far-fetched and unreasonable mission. But if His life and death and resurrection had proved anything to them, it proved that He could make a way. If He said they could do it, He would make sure they could do it.

And He'll make sure we are equipped to do it, too.

For you and for me—modern-day disciples—the command to be disciple makers is clear. Jesus's words tell us to go. They tell us to teach. They tell us to be part of spreading His gospel, helping other hungry believers transfer this same discipleship mentality that we've come to more fully understand into their minds and their hearts and their daily decisions. And they also tell us He will be there with us the whole time, "always, to the end of the age," to empower us, equip us, and encourage us to see the mission through. We can only fail by failing to obey.

But if we'll follow Him even in this—to give away what we've been given—we will find ourselves encouraged like *never before* to follow Him more passionately. And more personally.

This could be the key for the surge of growth and breakthrough you've been craving.

If you're starting to feel stuck inside your prayer closet, it's probably because it's time to welcome someone into your den or your dorm room, out to lunch or at the coffee shop—someone the Lord has sovereignly been working to pair with you—someone who has been praying for someone else who could show her what it really means to follow Christ.

Because when you're not just seeking the Lord for yourself but also taking the time to invest in someone else, it stirs your faith and ignites a renewed momentum and holy passion. And when you start to witness the same excitement for Him start to blossom in someone else as a result of what the Lord is pouring into you, there's no roof to contain the blessings and the benefits.

And so . . .

Go

Every single day, you and I are in position to impact other people for the glory of God and to invite them into a more intimate, more fervent relationship with Jesus Christ. If we will have eyes to see, ears to hear, and if we will have hearts that are sensitive to detect spiritual realities, the Lord will constantly send us opportunities to pass along the living truths of His everlasting kingdom to others.

For many, the temptation is to think the task of disciple-making is reserved for those who have seminary degrees on their walls or ministry microphones in their hands. We tend to think the command doesn't apply to us, that we're not qualified for it because we don't have the charisma and platform for it. But this couldn't be further from the truth. Remember, when Jesus first spoke these words, He was directing them to a motley crew of reformed fishermen, accountants, and other average joes, not to theologically trained religious thinkers. We are *all* called to this ministry as redeemed children of God, sent to tell "all nations" of our Savior. It is part and parcel of our own surrender. It's part of our privilege. It's part of our worship. It's part of our gratitude as believers in a God who has been gracious enough to make us His disciples as well.

"Go . . ."

In the original language, this single English word can be expanded to mean, *"As* you go." The implication is that the driving mission of making disciples is meant to be a continuous thread running throughout the regular rhythms of our everyday lives.

As we go through the day, we anticipate opportunities. We look for them. We stay on prayerful alert for them, keeping our heads on a swivel for them. We're not surprised but expectant that any encounter today could shimmer with holy and sacred potential, giving us opportunity to say something, do something, or be an example to others of what Jesus has made us and called us to be. Our set of tasks for the morning, our to-do list for the afternoon, are surrendered tools in His hand for wherever He says we should go, to whomever He puts in front of us.

Disciples recognize there's nothing of chance or happenstance within the spheres of influence we've been placed to engage. The meeting you're scheduled to lead, the child you're assigned to parent, the organization you've been entrusted to steward, the athletes you've recruited to coach, the employees you've been tasked to manage, or the neighbors you live near—it's all by design. All of it is layered with the anytime prospect of becoming a sacred interaction.

An "as you go" encounter.

The Bible is replete with "as you go" moments that God transformed into significant experiences. Young David, when he was not yet the mighty king of Israel, was sent by his father, Jesse, on an errand to serve his older brothers who were fighting on the front lines as part of Israel's army. "Take this half-bushel of roasted grain along with these ten loaves of bread for your brothers and hurry to their camp" (1 Sam. 17:17), like an ancient DoorDash driver delivering lunch orders. His objective was to take them this care package from home. "Check on the well-being of your brothers" (v. 18), then bring back word on how they were faring. Go, give, ask, come back, and report. That was the to-do list on his day's agenda.

How could David have known it would also be the day he met Goliath face-to-face on the battlefield and completed a holy assignment that would become a defining event of his lifetime.

And then there's Obadiah. He was a holy man determined to honor Yahweh and serve his people, the nation of Israel, even while being employed as an official of evil king Ahab. One morning, amid a devastating three-and-a-half-year drought, he showed up for work and received his assignment for the day: "Go throughout the land to every spring and to every wadi. Perhaps we'll find grass so we can keep the horses and mules alive and not have to destroy any cattle" (1 Kings 18:5). Those were his orders, to go look for anything green and growing.

How could Obadiah have known, while he was carrying out this mundane duty, Yahweh would sovereignly connect his path with the prophet Elijah, an encounter that would lead to two altars being built on Mount Carmel, with one of them licked up in fire by the power of Almighty God.

Or what about Ruth? She was a woman discouraged and disjointed from the only life she'd ever known, a young Moabite widow who had decided to follow her widowed Israelite mother-in-law, Naomi, home to Bethlehem. But even together, their prospects for having enough to live on were bleak. Desperate for food, she "happened" to end up (Ruth 2:3) in the nearby fields of a man named Boaz, hoping to collect enough grain for both Naomi and herself from the scattered strands that accidentally fell from the reapers' hands during harvest. This was how she intended to spend the day.

How could Ruth have known that this man, Boaz, would become her husband, with whom she would bear a child, a little boy by the name of Obed, whose son would be the same Jesse who sent his son David with a lunch basket to his brothers in the army? The same David who would become a giant slayer and a king.

A lot can happen "as you go."

⌇⌇

Jesus's lifestyle was the epitome of this. Think of the assignment on His mind as He was on His way to Jerusalem for the final time.

"See, we are going up to Jerusalem. The
Son of Man will be handed over to the chief
priests and the scribes, and they will con-
demn him to death. Then they will hand
him over to the Gentiles, and they will mock
him, spit on him, flog him, and kill him,
and he will rise after three days." (Mark
10:33–34)

No one has ever had so much on his plate, so much to
be preoccupied with. And yet . . .

While traveling to Jerusalem, he passed
between Samaria and Galilee. As he entered
a village, ten men with leprosy met him.
They stood at a distance and raised their
voices, saying, "Jesus, Master, have mercy
on us!"
When he saw them, he told them, "Go
and show yourselves to the priests." And
while they were going, they were cleansed.
(Luke 17:11–14, emphasis added)

Even with where Jesus was going—and with what He
was going there to do—He was still listening, He was
still looking, He was still anticipating the ongoing will
of His Father, on the lookout for people He could draw
toward Himself. This "village" he entered was not His

destination; He was on His way into the city. But this "as you go" moment was not just a fluke of good luck for ten lepers in need of what only Jesus could do. The *going* was as much on His schedule as the place He was heading.

How do we know? Because it had been His established habit to be alert to His Father's business on His way to many places.

- Once as Jesus "approached" the city of Jericho, a blind man heard He was "passing by." Above the raucous crowd noise, Jesus could hear the anguished voice of the man crying out for help. Jesus stopped, called him to come near, blessed him for his faith, and restored his sight (Luke 18:35–43).
- "On his way" to the town of Nain, Jesus saw a funeral procession in the distance. Coming through the city gate was a large crowd comforting a grieving widow, as pallbearers carried the coffin of her only son to his grave. Jesus "saw her" and "had compassion on her," drew near enough to touch the open casket, and the man sat up alive (Luke 7:11–17)!
- "While he was going" to the home of a man whose daughter was near death, Jesus

sensed a woman come up behind Him in
the crowd, thinking just by touching His
robe she might be cured of her blood disorder. Though His business with the syna-
gogue leader was urgent, He took time to
speak with this timid, faithful woman and
declare her healed of her disease (Luke
8:41–48).

This was simply His way. To watch and to listen. To
seek and to serve. To respond to people who were trying
to figure out what having faith in Him could do. And He
did it *on His way.*

John 4 describes a life-altering conversation Jesus
had with a woman who was drawing water from a well.
Verse 3 says Jesus had left Judea, heading north to Galilee,
and that "he had to travel through Samaria" (v. 4). *Had* to?
Yes—not simply because that's where the natural lines of
geography took Him but because that's where the supernatural leading of His Father's sovereignty had sent Him.

Even for so important a task as calling His first disciples, the Bible says it took place "as he passed alongside
the Sea of Galilee," where He saw Simon and Andrew
and invited them to follow Him. And then, "going on a
little farther," he came across another set of brothers—
James and John—whom He commissioned with the same
invitation (Mark 1:16–20). Appointing these men was

a primary objective that was crucial to His mission, yet even this important calling happened *as He went.*

The people Jesus met and ministered to in these seemingly unscheduled encounters were often shocked to find themselves in His presence, but Jesus was never surprised by theirs. Making these kinds of on-time, real-time connections is what He'd been sent to do. This was His purpose in being there. He was never more focused on getting to Point B than watching for Point A priorities to develop on the way.

And we, as His disciples, should travel with the same expectation. If we want to be like Jesus, if we want to reflect the heart of Jesus, if we want to express the compassion of Jesus—if we truly want to follow Jesus—we will make the "making of disciples" our new, overarching job description, even in the most informal, in-passing sorts of ways. We represent Him everywhere we go. Not just when we get there but all the time as we're going.

Is it possible you've been waiting until you "get there"—until you arrive at some theoretical destination, until you reach some level of theological knowledge or mastery—before you feel like you can be a useful disciple who is on mission to make other disciples? There's no need to wait any longer. Instead, remember His promise, "I am with you always"—every step of the way—to open your eyes to every opportunity and then empower you to excel in it.

As you go.

So I offer to you a prayer that I've incorporated into my own prayer life, to help stir your own focus toward disciple-making. Starting today, pray this:

Lord, open my spiritual eyes to see the opportunities You will give me to represent You to others today. Give me an unusual sensitivity to the places where You are already working and where You're inviting me to partner with You in the life of someone else. And give me an overflow of resources, both tangible (like money) and intangible (like time and patience) that will allow me to be the answer to someone else's prayer.

If you will begin to pray like this, I can assure you from my own personal testimony that you'll immediately begin to recognize a new pattern forming around you. You'll see that many of the things you used to call *interruptions* are actually divine *interventions* and holy *invitations* for you to partner with your Lord in His sovereign plans and purposes.

Baptize Them

Several years ago, I took an unforgettable trip to Israel. Every aspect of the journey through the Holy Land was spectacular, as you can imagine. The guide's explanation of historical sites and the biblical history connected to them was both fascinating and eye-opening.

One of the most memorable visits was to a village in Nazareth that had been rebuilt on ancient remains unearthed by archaeologists from deep underground. Workers in period dress had been hired to reenact many of the activities that would've been prevalent within the life of this community during the days of Christ. Vinedressers were tending vineyards. Watchmen were stationed on a watchtower overlooking the area. There was also a well-designed hut-like structure in which weavers were working with wool, demonstrating how these first-century artisans turned the raw material into useful threads and yarns on a pedal-driven spindle.

Once the wool was spun into yarn, the masterful weaver put specific ingredients into boiling pots of water—like saffron, pomegranate, walnuts, onion peels, or tree leaves—to create a certain hue in each container. She would then immerse whole lengths of the plain wool thread into the vats of hot liquid, baptizing them and converting them from neutral blandness into varied, vibrant colors.

The immersive process completely transformed the yarn. The goal behind this baptismal process wasn't just to get the material wet; it was to utterly change its identity so that it was no longer associated with the drab, dingy shade that had previously characterized it. The wool was new. It was fresh. It was useful. It was beautiful.

The biblical sacrament of water baptism for the believer is for this same purpose. It's a one-time obedient act of proclamation and reidentification. It's first an announcement to everyone who witnesses it that this person is not the same, now that she's believed in Christ, now that she's repented of her sins and been declared forgiven by her faith in the shed blood of Jesus. And then, the water dripping from her sleeves and hair and fingertips is emblematic of the new identity that is hers. Symbolically, she enters the water one way and emerges changed, different, and new.

Much like the new coloring of the wool is a recategorizing of its identity, water baptism is a picture of this same transformation. Listen to how the apostle Paul articulated it:

> Are you unaware that all of us who were baptized into Christ Jesus were baptized into his death? Therefore we were buried with him by baptism into death, in order that, just as Christ was raised from the dead by the glory of the Father, so we too may walk in *newness of life*. (Rom. 6:3–4, emphasis added)

As we take seriously Jesus's command to "baptize them," this will mean helping those we disciple to recognize and live in light of the identity shift that their water baptism signified. To help them realign their mindset, attitudes, and behaviors to reflect their new identity in the practical rhythms of life. To assist them in daily living out the reality of being dead to sin and alive to God. Growing into this "newness" of heart and mind, of soul and body that a believer is now able to experience. No longer going through the day as if their lives are still predicated by the old colors of their past. The child of God is new. She is free.

People desperately need to be discipled to understand what their baptism really means—that they are not only released from their sin but are also "released from the law, since we have *died* to what held us, so that we may serve in the *newness* of the Spirit and not in the *old* letter of the law" (Rom. 7:6, emphasis added). They are no longer forced to follow sin and no longer forced to follow the law. They are free now just to follow Jesus—not just because it's what we do but because it's aligned with who we are.

Changed. Baptized.

Into a newness of life.

As a disciple.

This is the light bulb of revelation you now have the privilege of igniting in the lives of other people "as you go" and "make disciples" who've been "baptized" into a new identity.

Look around. Who in your sphere needs to better understand this? Who are you encountering in the regular cadence of your day that you already do life with? It might be your children. (Definitely your children.) Never overlook the young disciples growing up right under your roof and the friends that often come over to play with them. But maybe it's a neighbor. Maybe it's a young woman or teenager in your church. Maybe it's a coworker, a fellow parent you frequently run into at ball practice, the lady who does your nails, even a stranger the Lord has led you into relationship with in some unusually interesting way.

Go.

Baptize them.

And . . .

Teach Them

At my home church in Dallas, my sister oversees an ongoing, weekly meeting for women called Life on Life. It's appropriately named because the goal of the gathering is not merely to hear God's Word taught but to receive practical guidance on how to implement it into daily life. It's "one life" rubbing up against another life through the sharing of truth and experience with each other. It's one person choosing to be vulnerable enough to share from her highs and lows, her triumphs and missteps, her joys and difficulties, allowing the others in her group to learn and benefit from what the Lord has shown her.

Because what good is knowing what God says without understanding what to do with it, how to be obedient to it? In real life?

This, too, is part of making disciples the way Jesus commanded us to do it. *By teaching.* Both the systematic teaching of God's truth as He's revealed it in Scripture, combined with the insight to be gleaned from people who've put His truth into practice. Or who, from time to time, have *not* put His truth into practice and have gathered valuable lessons the hard way. We can learn (and teach) from those experiences as well.

I'm convinced this is one of the critical components missing from the body of Christ today. Millions of people listen to the Bible being taught for an hour and a half in their Sunday meeting each week, but they get no personal, ongoing, "life on life" help beyond this time slot on their calendar. They wonder why they never make much progress in incorporating what they've learned into their daily life.

This is the reason: they haven't met someone willing to teach them, or they haven't been willing to be taught.

- Like a new father, who was raised by a
  single mother, being shown by another

man how to honor God in his parenting
role by putting the principles of Scripture
to work in his life.

- Like a young entrepreneur being coun-
seled by a seasoned businesswoman how
to cast vision, manage people, and implement effective strategy while applying
God's principles to her developing business ventures.

- Like a high school student who is navigating the unique pressures facing the current
generation of teenagers, being taken under
the wing of a twenty-something mentor.

- Like a young mother who wants to learn
how to effectively manage a home, find
balance in her schedule, and nourish her
family physically and spiritually, being
welcomed into the life of an empty nester
who has already walked this path.

At any point in each of our lives, we should be both
of these people at the same time—both *receiving* personal
teaching from an older, more mature disciple while also
giving personal teaching to a younger, maturing disciple.
Willing to give while also being willing, in humility, to
receive.

There's a balance and a bounty to be unearthed in both.

And when we ignore or avoid this aspect of discipleship because of the time investment involved or the fear of not being wise and grounded enough to speak with any authority to someone else, we short another of God's beloved children from a blessing and rob ourselves of one, too.

By choosing to sidestep and ignore this imperative, we put a choke hold of restriction on the fully surrendered, next-level degree of devotion we so want to experience with our Savior.

Listen to the hauntingly true words of Watchman Nee, a Chinese evangelist from the early twentieth century:

> Alone I cannot serve the Lord effectively, and he will spare me no pains to teach me this. He will bring things to an end, allowing doors to close and leaving me ineffectively knocking my head against a blank wall until I realize that I need the help of the Body as well as of the Lord. For the life of Christ is the life of the Body, and his gifts are given to us for work that builds up the Body.[6]

Don't receive Christ's Great Commission as an unwanted demand, as a threat to be avoided in a life too busy with other things. Embrace it, Beloved. There is abundant life here. There's a flowering of your purpose, an expansion to your capacity. There's a new depth of dependence on Jesus, as well as the new motivation for learning and growing in your knowledge of Him.

In shearing off any complicating extras that may be keeping you from investing your life in others, you'll find they've only been stealing from you and diminishing your life for all these years anyway. In losing them, you can finally stretch out to your full spiritual height and taste the rare joys of fulfilling your calling. You can walk in the unencumbered freedom of living for Christ and His kingdom alone.

We need you. There's for sure at least one person in your world right now who *really* needs what a disciple-to-discipler relationship with you could do for them. This connection could encourage the jump start to their faith that they've been dying to discover. And from there to many others.

- *Go* to them. Reach out to people in the name of Jesus.
- *Baptize* them. Help them enter into and live out a saved identity in Jesus.

- *Teach* them. Show them through example and explanation how to practically incorporate biblical truth into their everyday lives.

And then prepare for all the limits to come off the top of your surrendered heart for Jesus.

Surrendering All

Imitate me, as I also imitate Christ.
1 Corinthians 11:1

What are some of the places you routinely "go" that you
don't usually think of as having significant potential for
God to use? How could you more consistently surrender
these moments to Him?

_____

_____

_____

_____

_____

_____

_____

_____

_____

_____

_____

_____

_____

In what ways, if any, do you feel inadequate or unable to disciple another? Write down anything that comes to your mind, then take the time to offer these to the Lord.

_____

_____

_____

_____

_____

_____

_____

_____

_____

_____

_____

_____

_____

Use these words as a springboard for your own prayer time with the Lord right now. Talk with Him and journal what His Spirit is saying to you: *Lord, open my spiritual eyes to see the opportunities You will give me to represent You to others today. Give me an unusual sensitivity to the places where You are already working, and where You're inviting me to partner with You in the life of someone else. And give me an overflow of resources, both tangible and intangible that will allow me to be the answer to someone else's prayer.*

_____

_____

_____

_____

_____

_____

_____

_____

_____

_____

For Further Reading

Romans 10:14–17 • Colossians 1:28–29 • Titus 2:4–8

CHAPTER 8

Everything for Jesus

For the love of Christ compels us.

2 Corinthians 5:14

There are roughly 170 United States embassies scattered in different countries and continents throughout the world. These embassies represent America's interests even though they are situated on foreign soil, and they provide a safe haven for U.S. citizens who live there or may be traveling abroad. If an American is in trouble, the embassies will represent and enforce the laws of the United States on its citizens' behalf.

At the head of each embassy is a United States ambassador, a high-ranking diplomat who represents the interests and ideals of the American government—again, despite living and working on foreign ground. While every facet of their daily activities occurs within the country to which they've been assigned, they remain constantly aware of their purpose, as defined by the country they represent. They are no less ambassadors when doing the normal stuff of life—cooking dinner with their families, sharing an evening with their friends, or running errands—than when they are overseeing a meeting with foreign government officials. Ambassadors know who they are, they know where they come from, and they know what their assignment is. So every decision they make is informed by their overarching mission to represent the United States well. This means they consistently and intentionally acknowledge their allegiance to their homeland, even while being a resident in a foreign land. They don't mindlessly blend into their surroundings. They are *ambassadors*. In everything they do. Everywhere they go. Always.

And so are we.

As believers in Jesus, we are ambassadors of heaven's kingdom. We are situated on the foreign soil of a fallen earth, but this compromised version of it is not our home. We are *in* the world, but we are not "of the world" (John 17:14, 16). Instead of mixing in seamlessly with it, we must remain constantly aware that we are on assignment to represent the interests and ideals of the kingdom from which we've been sent. This means everywhere we go and in everything we do, we are ambassadors for Him. The assignment doesn't change depending on whatever else we are doing each day. We are always on mission. Everyone we meet, when they're around us for any length of time, should be able to tell who we are and what our assignment is, not because we're announcing it but because of the way we live out the ideals of our King and His kingdom.

This is what ambassadors do. This is who we are.

We are heaven's representatives, sent here with orders from home to follow. To go and teach and make disciples, just as Jesus has told us. To make more disciples like ourselves, who then go and make disciples of others. And this overarching umbrella can and should remain intact as we engage in the regular tasks of our regular lives. Our playing and working and organizing and entertaining shouldn't mask our role as ambassadors. They should provide organic opportunity to reveal and highlight it.

As I think back on the lives that have most impacted my own, I am in awe of how frequently I've been inspired and led into deeper discipleship by other people who were going about the natural rhythm of their lives while also keeping their kingdom assignment in clear view.

Yes, sometimes it has been by a person who was intentional about seeking me out (or me seeking them out) for the purpose of investing in my spiritual growth. We'd organize a specific time to get together; then we'd sit across from each other with Bibles open, preparing ourselves prayerfully to stare deeply into what God has said in His Word. Then we'd seek the Spirit's leading on how I should apply this to my own life. But at other times, discipleship has come in the form of an impromptu encounter with someone whose surrender to Christ was so complete that she just naturally oozed Christlikeness in whatever she was doing at the moment. Completely on the go and organic, yet no less biblical, no less impactful, no less necessary to my own maturation process.

Some who've discipled me have been people who serve God in full-time vocational ministry, but many of them—almost all of them, in fact—are people who've never needed a formal ministry title in order to feel motivated to invest in me, to help me (and many others like me) to grow and develop as a sincere disciple of Christ. Instead, they've just taken Romans 12:1 seriously: "Take your everyday, ordinary life—your sleeping, eating, going-to-work, and walking-around life—and place it before God as an offering" (MSG).

And I'm so glad they did.

Lynda

When I was a teenager, I often traveled with my parents on ministry trips. And frequently, when my father would be scheduled to preach at a conference, a young woman named Lynda would lead worship. She was ten or fifteen years older than I was, and she was already married. She certainly didn't need to concern herself with a teenage girl who was hanging around. Yet she would intentionally keep me close to her during those gatherings. She'd put her arm around me and welcome me to be by her side. I'd sit next to her. I'd share meals with her. She looked me in my eyes, asked me questions about my life, and was genuinely interested in my answer. The attention she paid to me as a young girl made me feel seen and valued.

One time, I remember being in the women's dressing room with her, right before she went out to sing before a large congregation. She was six months pregnant with her first child at the time, and she was still getting accustomed to having a rounded belly. I sat on a stool in the corner of the green carpeted room and watched as she adjusted her outfit to prepare for her upcoming time on the evening program.

When she faced the mirror to finish getting dressed, she casually talked about how important it was for her to make sure she was completely comfortable in her clothing before going out to minister to others. She didn't want anything uncomfortable or ill fitting to unnecessarily distract her from focusing on leading the attendees into God's presence. So she made sure there was nothing she would need to fidget with or adjust in the middle of her singing and sharing.

I watched the detail with which she made sure her clothing was modest and becoming, feminine but not flashy. Because not only did she want to remain personally undistracted herself, but she told me she also wanted to extend that same courtesy to the audience. They weren't there to see *her*; they were there to see *Him*. And if they were busy watching *her*—worried that she might trip over a skirt that was too long, grimacing about a blouse that was too low, or sidetracked by a strap that wouldn't stay put—their attention would be less focused on *Him*. There'd be less single-mindedness for them to devote to hearing what the Spirit might want to say.

I can't tell you how many times, in the decades that have passed, I've thought back to that single, solitary moment of discipleship. The memory of seeing her take a calm and determined effort to make sure her clothing was appropriate and undistracting left a lasting imprint on me. It has informed my fashion choices ever since then, particularly when I'm ministering to others. Lynda taught me as a young teenage girl the importance of not being unnecessarily distracted by issues of self so that I can keep the main thing, the main thing. And when I'm standing in front of others to share the Scriptures, the main thing isn't me. It's Him. I never want what I'm wearing to be either *too much* or *too little*, to make me uncomfortable or distract those I'm serving.

I learned this from Lynda, as well as many other meaningful pieces of spiritual insight from times when she and her husband, Michael, invited me into their home and spent time talking with me about their regular lives and their love for the Lord. *She discipled me.*

Kim

Kim was a single woman who worked in a corporate office environment and led a full and interesting life. Our shared birthday was the common ground that led us into a yearslong friendship, despite the fact that she was more than a decade older than me. She would occasionally whisk me away from my regularly scheduled junior-high activities, inviting me out for some "girl time," which, I can see now, was really just a disguise for discipleship time.

We would discuss my teenage-sized problems while we walked the mall, went swimming, or visited other entertaining places, like the Fort Worth Water Gardens. At the time, I thought we were just friends—how cool, being personal buddies with a grown woman like that!— but, now in hindsight, I realize Kim was intentionally investing in me. We would talk about life, how she was navigating aspects of her career and the dating scene as a spectacularly gorgeous and surrendered single woman. She would share age-appropriate insights, give me sound advice for my own life, and allow me access into her world. *She discipled me.*

Mrs. Echols

Mrs. Echols had been a successful businesswoman for many years and was also a longtime member of our home church. During my teenage years, she signed up to be a small group leader for the youth and then invited a group of girls, which included me, into her life for discipleship.

This clever, creative woman would consistently open up her home to this little handful of girls, where we'd meet with her outside of a normal Sunday school setting, without all the dressy formality of church and classrooms and folding chairs. She would think up engaging projects for us to do together, like cooking delicious dinner dishes or molding our own ceramic pots while teaching us how the Holy Spirit was molding us into Christ's image.

By taking time she didn't have—time she certainly wasn't required to spend on the young people in her church—she fostered a beautiful friendship between us girls in a place where we could feel safe and affirmed. *She discipled me.*

CeCe

My parents once took me to see the brother-sister singing team of BeBe and CeCe Winans in concert. I loved every minute of the evening, and I was over-whelmed with excitement when I learned our family had been invited to an after-concert dinner at the host's home with these gospel artists. I'd never met this dynamic duo before, and I couldn't believe I would get the opportunity to be in such close proximity to them.

As you might imagine, I was completely starstruck. Here I was, just a teenager, and CeCe was the undisputed queen of gospel music. The first thing that caught my eye after we'd arrived for dinner was this amazing woman, who had just mesmerized an audience of thousands for two full hours, stooping down on the den floor, playing with her toddler-age son and daughter. The rest of the grown-ups kept talking and enjoying a refined adult soiree until it was finally time for everyone to head into the formal dining room where dinner would be served. I remember the host going over to CeCe, assuring her that someone would safely watch her kids while she came and ate with the others.

I don't know exactly what she said in response or what specific reasons she had, but I'll never forget watching this mother make the decision to stay with her children on the floor, eating with them on paper plates instead of opting for adult conversation around beautifully arranged china place settings. I watched her out of the corner of my eye throughout that whole night, seeing the pure contentment on her face from choosing to spend time with her own kids rather than eat dinner with acquaintances.

Many years later, when Jerry and I began traveling with our children for ministry opportunities, this offhand observation of CeCe Winans from that night became a compass marker for me. During our sons' formative years, my chief aim was seeking to create time and opportunity

to spend intentional time with them, and I would orchestrate our trip to accommodate that. My goal became to
minimize my separation from them, being sure our boys
were with us as much as possible. And, to think, the Lord
used one encounter with this gifted musical artist (and
devoted mother) to show me it really could be done. Her
commitment to her family and her integrity in honoring
her own priorities marked me. She didn't know it then,
and it would be many decades later until I could tell her
that *she discipled me.*

Maria

Maria was an accomplished woman who'd built a
solid and respected career in television. As I entered college to study broadcast journalism—which, at that point
in my early twenties, I was bound and determined to
make my life's work—she gave me practical direction on
how to cultivate a steady career in the field.

She taught me about having poise on camera and
how to articulate my words. She encouraged me to start
sharpening my skills and beefing up my résumé by par-
ticipating in any low-budget projects I could find. She
personally photographed my first headshots, taking on
the role of makeup artist and teaching me everything she
knew about the importance of color choices, lighting, and
scope for an appropriate biographical photograph. She

also helped me prepare for auditions. And when my first efforts didn't translate into solid work, she was there to encourage me not to give up, to keep learning, even from the setbacks.

Best of all, she told me how she'd navigated the hardened, cutthroat media industry from a Christian perspective and how she'd been able to use her influence and platform to demonstrate the difference her faith made in the work she did. *She discipled me.*

Tammy

When I was a young wife and mom, I wanted all the help I could get to learn how to cultivate the kind of home that would be a sanctuary for my husband and our growing family. And I'd always been amazed at Tammy's spectacular homemaking skills. Quite frankly, they are like none I'd ever witnessed before or since.

So I was thrilled when she was willing to share practical tips on some of the finer points of homemaking. She would send me home with deliciously easy-to-make, mouth-watering recipes (some of which I still use to this day), as well as little hints she'd learned through the years for decorating on a dime. When I would mention to her some of the details of her home that I found the most intriguing, she'd let me take photos of them. Then she'd give me instructions on how to duplicate what I loved so much about her house in my own, in cost-effective ways.

But Tammy's flair for cooking and creating impressive table spreads was hardly designed for being showy and pretentious. She taught me the importance of creating a space where everyone who crossed our threshold could immediately sense the peace and presence of God. She wanted me to see hospitality as a gift, a ministry, that increased the possibility of people experiencing His tender love and care while in our home. She even taught me how to properly entertain our guests by letting me come be a guest of hers and her family overnight, just to show me how she did it. Tammy allowed me to soak in not only her talented teaching but her devotion for Christ so that I could seek to craft our home after the same design and purpose. *She discipled me.*

Anne

In my mid-twenties, when the Lord was just beginning to reveal His purposes and plans for my life, Anne Graham Lotz graciously invited me to travel with her for a season, to try out my sea legs in ministry, letting me emcee during some of her events. Those experiences made a significant impact on the entire trajectory of my life.

Being up close with her, and with the other women who shared the platform with her, allowed me to see what it looked like not only to proclaim God's Word with clarity, precision, authority, and passion to others but also to live the kind of life *off*stage that displayed personal character and integrity to the ministry. I was like a fly on the wall in those greenrooms—with people like Kay Arthur, Sheila Bailey, Jill Briscoe, and others—witnessing the integrity they modeled in their conversation and their conduct, in hidden spaces where most people never saw them.

Overhearing some of those conversations was among the most impactful experiences of my life, being mentored as a young woman, just by being in the same space. More than anything, those years under her wing taught me that real ministry is simply the outpouring of someone's own authentic relationship with Jesus. Ms. Anne, as I still endearingly call her to this day, helped me see it in real life. *She discipled me.* And these decades later, she still does.

John and Trina

And then there are John and Trina Jenkins, the couple to whom this book is dedicated. Jerry and I were somewhere within the first five years of our marriage when we met them. I'll never know all the reasons, but the Jenkins chose to endear their hearts to us as a young couple. For the duration of our twenty-five-year marriage (and counting!) they have made it their business to attend to the health of our family and ministry. They ask us hard questions and then require of us honest answers about the often unaddressed dynamics that can cause a marriage, family, and ministry to implode if left to time and chance.

As we raised our children, John and Trina were our sounding board, giving us faithful feedback on how to make solid decisions for each stage of growth in our sons' lives. Having raised six unique children, who each had varying personalities, interests, and hobbies, their perspective and insight have been invaluable to us. They've invited us into their home more times than I can count and have spent more hours with us than I can calculate, giving us the opportunity to see the beautiful chaos of raising a family while keeping Christ at the center. Looking back through the years, Jerry and I know for sure the stability of our family through the ups and downs of our lives can largely be attributed to these mentors' influence and investment in us.

They discipled us.

৽

I could go on with more examples like these. In each season of my life, faithful believers have taken time to disciple me and invest in my maturity. They deliberately viewed their own areas of industry and personal interest as opportunities to impact others for the Lord's sake. They were alert to the people He'd organically placed around them. They didn't discount the sovereign hand of God in strategically entrusting them with their specific platform and then arranging their paths to intersect with specific people.

To them, there was no separation between the sacred part of their lives and the secular. They understood, as Christ's disciple and ambassador, that their entire lives should reflect His nature and underscore His purposes. I'm sure they never knew all the times someone like me simply caught them in the midst of just living their lives—exhibiting integrity, excellence in their craft, and deference to their Father's will—and was inspired, course corrected, and instructed on her own path because of it. The power of their simple testimonies spoke something about Christ to the other person that not even a whole sermon series might communicate. They weren't doing it for a paycheck. They weren't doing it because people expected it. They just considered themselves on mission for God wherever He'd placed them—His ambassadors on duty—asking Him, "Lord, who have you placed close to me today that I can encourage to live in a way that honors You?"

A spectacular example of the kind of disciple-making I'm talking about is displayed in the movie *The Forge*, in which I had the honor of playing the role of Cynthia, single mother to a nineteen-year-old young man named Isaiah.

When the film opens, Isaiah is floundering. His attitude is curt and ungrateful, his heart is hard, and the outlook for his life appears dim. Cynthia is frustrated by his lack of respect. She doesn't feel like he appreciates all she's had to endure and sacrifice to give him as good a life as possible. She's also discouraged because she recognizes that no matter how hard she's worked or how successful she's been as a mother to him, she's never been able to provide Isaiah some of the nuances he's needed in a father. And never can. So she asks the Lord to bring "surrogate fathers" into his life, men who will take an interest in him, mentor him. *Disciple him.*

That's where Joshua Moore comes in. He's basically a disciple disguised as a businessman. Though he's the owner of a thriving company, he's always watching closely to see who the Lord might bring into his path. Because to him, every encounter—particularly with a younger man like Isaiah—is an opportunity for discipleship.

On the day Isaiah comes into his place of business applying for a part-time job, Mr. Moore runs into him in the front lobby. Isaiah, unaware he's speaking with his potential employer, is moody and ill-mannered, and yet the CEO is not deterred, recognizing in this encounter a holy opportunity. He decides on the spot to offer Isaiah a job, but then he goes a step further by asking the young man to meet with him weekly a few minutes before work—a job, *plus*. Is Isaiah interested? Not really. But since he needs the work and needs the money, and since these are the terms he's been given, he accepts.

Over breakfast burritos and cinnamon rolls, the older man begins an ongoing series of conversations with his young protégé, giving Isaiah advice on everything from character to college choices, from finances to family matters. He challenges him, corrects him, advises him. He allows him to see what it looks like to be in business while serving Jesus with abandon.

Pretty soon, Isaiah's initial hesitance is worn down. He becomes intrigued by this man who's taken such a pointed interest in him and who truly lives out the biblical principles he teaches. Eventually, Isaiah's entire perspective and life are changed because of Joshua's determined, godly influence on him. He develops into the kind of aspiring leader his mentor—and his God—have been training him to be.

This is discipleship.

And this should be you. And me. We've each been given unique tools, experiences, and opportunities that make us valuable as disciplers. As we ongoingly surrender ourselves and our whole lives to Him, we will find that every part of our journey and individuality is useful in sovereignly pairing us with others who need godly influence and instruction.

Maybe you've lived the bulk of your Christian life still under the impression that surrendering yourself to Him mostly just means stopping the bad stuff you've been doing, that the big goal of being a Christian is getting the sin out of your life. That's certainly a key part of it.

But even this, if that's all you seek to do, is to limit what God wants to accomplish with your life. He's chosen you to surrender everything—*I Surrender All*—so that everything He's given you to steward is His now to use and bless and multiply.

There's so much more out there for you than just wrestling with and worrying about your sins. Your Father wants you thriving as His child, bearing the fruit He alone is able to grow in you so that He can use it to feed others, so that His kingdom can grow, so that His children can mature, so that His will may "be done on earth as it is in heaven" (Matt. 6:10).

Come, bringing everything.

Come, bringing all.

Come, be His surrendered disciple.

୧୨

Some of my favorite discipleship stories come from those early chapters in the book of Acts, when the Holy Spirit came in holy power upon the first believers in Jesus, and the newly born Christian church began putting down roots into the fresh soil of fresh faith.

Think with me of that time when the established religious leaders of the day were becoming annoyed by the widespread impact this renegade group—*these ambassadors of Jesus*—were having on the community. They had surrendered their all and were encouraging others to do the same. They were evangelizing. They were making new disciples. And the Spirit was empowering them to do such a good job of it that the old-guard culture was feeling threatened.

Acting within what they believed to be their authority, the Jewish leaders attempted to chop off the head. They seized Peter and John—known friends of Jesus— who appeared to be the ringleaders and pressured them with the risk of severe consequences if they didn't stop telling people Jesus had risen from the dead, if they didn't put a stop to this alarming escalation of converts who were trying to change the way religion worked (see Acts 4:1–18).

Truly, that's what had been happening. These first followers weren't just attending the standard religious gatherings; they were becoming everyday disciples, far beyond the limits of sacred performance. They were devoted not only to the apostle's teaching that they were hearing but to "fellowship," to the "breaking of bread" (Acts 2:42), to the daily interactions with other believers that invited Christian faith to change their whole behavior.

They were so committed to disciple-making that they made radical lifestyle changes to prioritize it, like selling off their possessions and using the money to care for others' needs, like not even considering their property their own anymore. They were willing to surrender their hold on material things so that more and more people could hear and be blessed by the good news of Jesus.

Word had gotten out, all right. The Jewish Sanhedrin, after a lengthy period of questioning and conferring over the troubling case of Peter and John, allowed them to be released but only under the stipulation that they not "speak or teach at all in the name of Jesus" (Acts 4:18). The church, hearing Peter and John's telling of it upon their return home, immediately began praying as one body, saying, "Lord, consider their threats, and grant that your servants may speak your word with all boldness, while you stretch out your hand for healing, and signs and wonders are performed through the name of your holy servant Jesus" (vv. 29–30).

At this point, they were such a Spirit-filled, disciple-making dynamo that nothing could stop them from wanting others to experience what Christ had done in them and what Christ could do in every person's life who believed in Him and became His disciple. Nothing had the power to dissuade them from telling this story or from

being on one common journey of faith with their brothers
and sisters.

Fear? No.

Business? No.

Society's expectations? No.

Scheduled appointments? No.

Other pressing priorities? No.

Everyday demands? No.

Personal interests? No.

Public opinion? No.

They were all-in, all together on this. They were
committed to making whatever surrender was required,
not only to live for Jesus themselves but to encourage and
instruct others on how to do the same. They were determined to stand up for Christ against all outside attempts
to minimize or belittle Him, as well as against all internal
logic that questioned or doubted their unfettered devotion
to Jesus.

They believed what you and I are still called by Christ
to believe. Discipleship means *all* of Him, interacting
with *all* the things we have, and with *all* the things we
do, until everything in our life is both informed and
impacted by Jesus: the way we think, the way we act, the
way we respond and reach out to other people, the way
we budget our time and treasures, and the way we make
our decisions.

When His first-century followers did this, the church grew by leaps and bounds. Disciples multiplied. People and families were generationally transformed. The Spirit of God equipped them with so much power and confidence and firsthand experience that they stopped doubting whether they could reach "all nations." Yes, they could. In Christ they could. And the way He'd chosen to do it was through the incredible simplicity of investing one surrendered life into another.

We're here because they did it. We're here because there's nothing any follower of Christ has ever given over to the Lord and fully entrusted to Him, completely relinquishing their control of it, that hasn't ended up being multiplied exponentially into a life-giving blessing, both in the present and in the future.

Surrender all, beloved disciple.

All that you are and all that you will be.

And be assured that He Himself will water and increase every seed you sow in your own life and in the lives of those you touch. May the sacred words the early church prayed for the first apostles in Acts 4:29–20 undergird us in this life until we both see Him face-to-face:

> "Lord, . . . grant that your servants may
> speak your word with all boldness, while
> you stretch out your hand for healing, and

signs and wonders are performed through
the name of your holy servant Jesus."

In Jesus's name.
The One who makes surrender worth it.
Amen.

Surrendering All

So we are ambassadors for Christ, as though
God were making His appeal through us;
we [as Christ's representatives] plead with
you on behalf of Christ to be reconciled to God.
2 Corinthians 5:20 AMP

List the people whose examples have most influenced the trajectory of your life for the glory of God. Did they disciple you directly or was their impact indirect?

_____

_____

_____

_____

_____

_____

_____

_____

_____

What experiences, passions, giftings, and spiritual insight has the Lord given you that provide you a unique vantage point through which His glory can be reflected through you to others?

_____

_____

_____

_____

_____

_____

_____

_____

_____

_____

_____

_____

_____

Prayerfully ask the Lord to highlight several people who are already in your sphere of influence. How can you disciple them in a way that is manageable for your lifestyle?

_____

_____

_____

_____

_____

_____

_____

_____

_____

_____

_____

_____

_____

_____

_____

For Further Reading

Acts 1:8 • Ephesians 4:1–3 • Hebrews 3:12–14

About the Author

Priscilla Shirer's voice rings with raw power and clarity throughout the nation and the world. Whether through her speaking ministry, her bestselling books and Bible studies, or on a movie screen—most recently in *The Forge*—her primary ambition is to lift up Jesus and equip His people to live victoriously. Her writings include series on biblical characters like *Jonah: Navigating a Life Interrupted*; *Elijah: Faith and Fire*; and *Gideon: My Weakness, His Strength*, as well as topical studies like *The Armor of God*. She has also authored a four-part fiction adventure series called The Prince Warriors, as well as award-winning, bestselling titles like *Fervent* (ECPA Christian Book of the Year), *The Resolution for Women*, and *Discerning the Voice of God*. She and her husband, Jerry, lead Going Beyond Ministries near Dallas, Texas, where they spend most of their time trying to satisfy the appetites of their three rapidly growing young adult sons.

Notes

1. https://www.bbc.com/culture/article/20220413-onoda-the-man-who-hid-in-the-jungle-for-30-years, accessed January 28, 2024.

2. Dietrich Bonhoeffer, *Discipleship* (Minneapolis, MN: Fortress, 2015), 50.

3. Elisabeth Elliot, *Be Still My Soul* (Grand Rapids, MI: Revell, 2017), 51.

4. C. S. Lewis, *Mere Christianity* (New York: Macmillan, 1943), 190.

5. Lewis, *Mere Christianity.*

6. Watchman Nee, *The Normal Christian Life* (Wheaton, IL: Tyndale, 1977), 217.

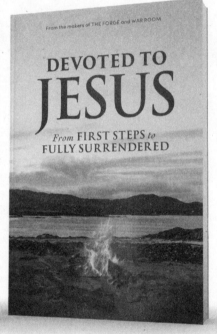

Other books *from*
Priscilla Shirer

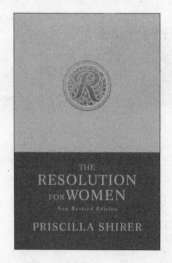

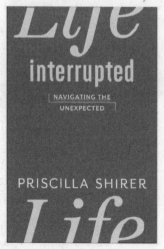

These and more available where books are sold.

Bible studies *from* Priscilla Shirer

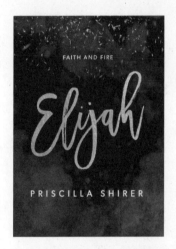

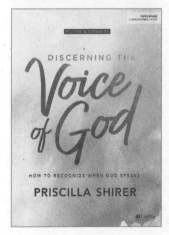

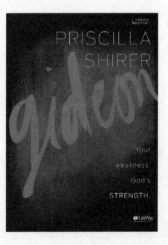

These and more available where books are sold.